IMAGES OF
DEFIANCE

IMAGES OF
DEFIANCE

South African resistance posters of the 1980s

The Poster Book Collective
South African History Archive

Ravan Press – Johannesburg

Dedication

Many of those involved in the production of posters in this book were grassroots members of organisations, identified only as 'com' or comrade. Some later went into hiding, others ended up in jail, or fled the country. Some died – killed in one of the confrontations with the state which have characterised our struggle. This book is dedicated to these unsung heroes, whose names are only known to those very close to them.

Produced by the Posterbook Collective
of the South African History Archive
P O Box 31719
Braamfontien
2017 South Africa

Published by Ravan Press
P O Box 31134
Braamfontein
2017 South Africa

Repro by Fotoplate
Cape Town
Printing by Clyson Printers
Cape Town

First published 1991

ISBN 0 86975 421 1

Contents

Foreword

In looking at these posters produced by the democratic movement in the 1980s, I find I have to be very careful in commenting on them. This is our collective work, of which I am naturally very proud. It would therefore be very easy to exaggerate, to overstate my own feelings about them. Having said that, I nevertheless acknowledge feelings of great pride, that in spite of all the difficulties our people have had to face, they were able to produce such work. It is very encouraging, especially to people of my generation, to know that the ideas for which many of us have sacrificed are very much alive and embodied in this collection of posters.

Posters can be a very beautiful form of propaganda. They are a powerful way of conveying information, provided they are simple and to the point. And the posters issued by the democratic movement have been very effective. Of course, it was not possible, in prison, to keep pace with all the posters that were issued, but we were very aware of them. It was clear to us that a lot of material was being produced by people's organisations in our country.

One way in which we could see the effect of posters was the change in the perceptions and in the level of political consciousness of the young people who came to prison. We realised that the propaganda that was being issued in the form of posters and other material contributed a great deal to the sharpening of people's perceptions and developing their ability to articulate their ideas and aspirations.

Posters were used back in the 1950s too, but not to such a degree. There are now better facilities for producing them, and there is more expertise amongst the activists themselves. It's a continuation of the same tradition, but today poster propaganda has become much more part of our struggle than in the past.

In the future, in a new and post-apartheid society, the usefulness of posters will continue to be as great as it is at the present moment. This tradition will not come to an end merely because we are free. Moreover, the use of posters will not be confined to political organisations only. Other disciplines also rely on posters to get their messages across, and they will continue to do so.

Posters can be very useful as an educational medium in a society like ours. They may even have to be used much more than now, as a means of reaching the people on development issues like literacy, health and so on. Many people do not want to read long dissertations on issues that affect their lives. They would like to see something that is brief and to the point, something to keep in the memory, take home and act on. Posters fulfil that demand very well.

The 1980s was the decade of poster production in South Africa. This book is a welcome contribution, recording as it does this important element in the history of our struggle.

Nelson Rolihlahla Mandela

Preface

Plans to produce a book of South African resistance posters were first made in 1987. It soon became clear, however, that working openly on such a project was not possible, because of the State of Emergency and other repressive actions by the state.

The posters themselves had to be kept in safe places known only to a few, and those working on the book had to meet secretly in order to protect the book and themselves. After media restrictions were introduced, the book's very existence had to be denied, even to friends and comrades, as involvement in the project was technically an offence in terms of the new regulations. At one point, contingency plans were made to publish the book anonymously and outside the country.

As a result, the project has taken four long years to complete. In some respects, this has proved to be an advantage. Who in 1987 would have thought that by 1991, the ANC and other organisations would be unbanned, Nelson Mandela and other leaders would be released from prison, and the first tentative steps towards a democratic South Africa finally taken? Who would have believed that the book could not only be freely published and sold, but that it would take its place on South African bookstands, next to publications issued by the African National Congress and the South African Communist Party? What better time to bring out a book celebrating the posters which played a part in achieving these victories?

Another advantage is that in 1991 we have many more posters to choose from than we had in 1987. In addition, we are able to reflect more fully the decade of the UDF, the MDM and the mass struggles that led to the momentous events of 1990.

The posters are divided into six categories. This was done to make the book more accessible and manageable for the reader, and to highlight some of the major areas of struggle in which the democratic movement engaged the apartheid regime – politics, labour, community, education, militarisation and repression, and art and culture.

There is an unavoidable overlap between the different sections in the book. Certain posters could have been placed in more than one section and we had to make a choice in this regard. Such an overlap is not surprising considering the close relationship between the different issues that make up the fabric of the struggle in South Africa.

We have made no attempt to analyse or offer a critique of the posters. We present the collection to the reader as part of the process of recording the history of various elements of the struggle.

This is not a comprehensive collection. Firstly, the posters are all issued by only one of the broad political tendencies in South Africa. The South African History Archive (SAHA), which is the custodian of the posters, collects material from all groupings, regardless of political persuasion. In its holdings and in its regular publication *History in the Making*, SAHA attempts to reflect the perspective of all players in the South African political arena.

However, in this book we have only included posters from organisations broadly associated with the Congress movement. Posters were produced by other groupings, but by far the majority were issued by organisations which were part of, or sympathetic to, the political tradition embraced by the UDF, COSATU and the ANC. The decision of the compilers of the book, the Posterbook Collective, to limit the selection of posters in this way is their own and does not necessarily reflect any opinion held by SAHA.

We have selected approximately 320 posters out of the almost 2 000 in SAHA's collection. This was done, reluctantly, because of practical and financial restraints.

We faced a dilemma when selecting posters for the book. How should we choose the 'best' posters? What does 'best' mean? Is it the 'best art', the 'best techniques', the most important message, the most attractive pictures, the brightest colours? We decided the criteria had to include whether a poster accurately reflected the times, and whether it captured in its words, images, its design, shape or colours, a significant moment in our struggle. The posters in this book are therefore not necessarily all fine examples of art, technique, imagery, design or rhetoric. They are reflections of a people and their fight for justice, liberation and peace.

Those who produced the posters did so in a collective spirit as part of their contribution to the struggle. In the case of posters which were designed by an individual rather than a group, we have not included the name of the designer: the purpose of the book is to celebrate that collective spirit and not to draw attention to individuals.

We have tried to be accurate in recording the origins of the posters, their date of publication, and the reasons why they were produced. We apologise for any errors in this difficult task.

The text which begins each category of posters provides readers with a broad overview of the issues reflected in the content of the posters, but is are not intended as a complete history of the struggle in South Africa.

This book is a celebration of our struggle: the victories and sacrifices, the commitment and dedication, and the making of posters.

It is also a celebration of the people who made the book possible. This includes those involved in the making of the posters as well as those who contributed to the production of the book itself.

The postermakers

One of the objectives of the workshops which produced most of the posters was training, and so organisations were encouraged to send the same people regularly so that, through this continuity, skills could be properly shared.

But how does one extract what appears to be a normal and logical commitment from people living under abnormal conditions? Many of the people involved in producing the posters were anonymous grassroots members of various organisations, identified only as 'com' or 'comrade'. Most came only once, some later went into hiding, others ended up in jail, or fled the country. Many are dead, killed in one of many confrontations with the state. Some came in to produce posters or T-shirts commemorating the death of a comrade, only to fall victim themselves soon afterwards.

The book is dedicated to these unsung heroes, whose names will probably only ever be known by those very close to them. Without them the posters in these pages would never have been produced.

We acknowledge the consistent support given to poster production by the leadership of the United Democratic Front and other structures of the democratic movement. We thank those funding agencies around the world who recognised the importance of poster making and provided financial support. This support continued even during those dark days when it was impossible to provide the funders with progress reports because of the level of repression directed at the democratic movement. We must also mention those commercial printers and repro houses willing to take the risks involved in producing posters, T-shirts and other propaganda material for our organisations.

Contributors to the book

Our appreciation must first go to those who had the foresight to begin collecting posters from the very beginning. They made the compilation of this book possible. This process of collecting was not without danger. The state saw posters as subversive, and the security police kept a constant look-out for the production and distribution of such media. Activists were beaten up or jailed simply because they were found with posters and leaflets in their cars and homes, or caught putting up posters in the clandestine darkness of night. In our collection there are copies of posters which were confiscated, and later returned, by the police. These carry the date of confiscation and the signature of the confiscating officer.

We are also grateful to the owner of the building in which the posters were secretly stored. He not only allowed us to keep the posters there in spite of the dangers, but maintained a consistent, low rental for the office for the four years that we used it.

We also thank those who contributed to the work of producing the book:
❏ the writers who contributed the text;
❏ the editors who helped us to produce the final draft;
❏ the individuals and organisations who provided copies of posters, especially Community Arts Project (CAP) and Media Archives Project (MAP) an offshoot of Screen Training Project (STP);
❏ South African History Archive (SAHA) and the Popular History Trust (PHT);
❏ South African Labour Bulletin for the use of its facilities;
❏ all those who provided photographic services;
❏ the various donors who provided funds for production of the book;
❏ Ravan Press, who waited, and waited...
❏ all those who encouraged and supported us through the long years which finally gave birth to this book.

All work has been done voluntarily and no individual will receive any financial return from the sale of the book. The subisidies will ensure that the book can be sold at a price which is more affordable, particularly to those who produced some of the posters. Any royalties and profits will go to the South African History Archive, which is now the custodian of the poster collection. ❏

The Posterbook Collective

Emilia Potenza
Marlene Powell
Charlotte Schaer
Judy Seidman
Morice Smithers

Making posters in South Africa

'To speak to the people by means of posters, to address that large number who do not even read cheap newspapers, is a revolutionary method...'
From The Palette and the Flame
a book of Spanish Civil War posters

Making posters in South Africa

Shattering the silence

'**As the sun set** and darkness crept into the dusty hall, people around us lit candles so that we could continue printing. While pulling the squeegies across the mesh, we noticed that local residents had crowded outside every window of the long, narrow room, trying to see what was happening. When we went out into the fading evening light to wash the screens off at the nearby communal tap, youngsters followed us, looking, touching, asking questions.

'This was the Lesedi Silkscreen Workshop (lesedi meaning light) in Huhudi, a black township in the Northern Cape that was fighting for its very existence. The government wanted to move the people to one of apartheid's bantustans, a backwater that the people of Huhudi saw as a wasteland of starvation and death.

'Members of the township's youth organisation and civic association had come to the Screen Training Project in Johannesburg to make posters to take back to their community. But one of STP's aims was to encourage communities to set up their own production units. We wanted people to produce, in their own areas, the posters and T-shirts that proclaimed their struggle for freedom. So we welcomed the request of the Huhudi community that we should help them set up their own workshop.

'The people of Huhudi started printing posters at the Lesedi workshop in 1985. The reaction of the state was swift. The workshop was petrol-bombed, some activists were detained, others fled the country. The States of Emergency imposed after 1985 eventually forced Lesedi to close.

'The attack on the poster workshop was part of a general clamp-down on political activity in the township as the state tried to force the residents to move and the people resisted. But the Huhudi community stood firm. Finally, after years of struggle, the government conceded that Huhudi could remain where it was. People's power had won, though not without cost.'

1 1985. One of the posters produced by the people of Huhudi in their struggle against forced removal.
Source: South African History Archive, Johannesburg

The poster movement in South Africa

The story of political posters in the 1980s is the story of the people and organisations that produced them. The posters in this book were not produced by an artistic elite, but by the people of South Africa. They reflect a grassroots vision of the struggles of the present and hopes for the future. They were produced in the face of enormous odds, ranging from a basic lack of skills and resources to outright bannings, detentions, and sometimes death.

The South African government force-fed the ideology of apartheid to all South Africans, black and white. The education system, the church, the military, the electronic and print media, and various cultural organisations, together churned out a steady diet of racist and supremacist theories. Even institutions not controlled by the state bowed to the constraints of the apartheid system: newspapers which questioned apartheid were either censored or banned, private educational institutions were closed down or denied the funds to operate.

At the same time, apartheid policies deprived communities of the opportunity to produce their own media. Bantu education left most people illiterate or semi-literate. With few exceptions, formal arts training was restricted to a small, privileged, and overwhelmingly white, middle class.

Deliberate state impoverishment and underdevelopment of townships and rural areas ensured that resources for media production – even such basic requirements as electricity – were out of reach for most communities.

The emerging grassroots community structures of the 1980s used posters, banners, leaflets, T-shirts, lapel badges, flags, stickers and graffiti in their fight to loosen the grip of apartheid ideas. By producing their own media, however unsophisticated, organisations claimed their right to be heard.

The posters in this book demonstrate their determination to win that right. Each challenges the state's attempt to hammer people into ideological submission. As a whole, they paint a picture of the popular struggle which reached its peak with the Defiance Campaign of 1989, leading finally to the unbanning of the African National Congress and other organisations, and the release of Nelson Mandela and his fellow political prisoners.

2 c1941. During the war, black South Africans volunteered to join the fight against Hitler, but they were not allowed to carry guns. *Source: South African Library, Cape Town*

Posters and poster culture in South Africa

Since the beginning of the 20th century in South Africa, posters have been used for commercial advertising and political propaganda. The most widespread political use was of the 'portrait of the candidate' type for whites-only elections.

During the Second World War, the government followed European trends of using posters to stir up patriotism and to raise money. But posters were also produced by the Communist Party of South Africa and by Medical Aid for Russia, a support group which collected money for the Soviet Union's war effort.

The extent to which posters were used as part of the very intense anti-apartheid struggles of the 1950s is not clear. It would seem that placards, banners and leaflets were more common.

Public mass protest and the use of graphics declined after the suppression of the ANC and PAC in 1960. By the end of that decade, the major source of poster production appears to have been university campuses. Student politics in the 1960s, especially among whites, reflected aspects of the militancy of campuses in Europe and the United States, which included the use of political posters. While distribution of these posters was mostly restricted to the campuses, their subject matter often dealt with major national issues. But one of the only known collections of these posters was destroyed in a mysterious fire which gutted a floor of the students' union building at Wits University in the early 1980s.

In the 1970s, trade unions re-emerged as a major force in South Africa. But they only began to use posters regularly in the latter part of the decade. Other organisations occasionally produced posters during this period. The black consciousness groups, the most vocal internal political force at the time, appear not to have used the medium much. The student uprising of 16 June 1976 seems to have relied upon individually-made placards and banners rather than printed posters. On the other hand, several posters commemorated the death in detention in 1977 of black consciousness leader, Steve Biko.

Therefore, although posters were used in various ways in the past, the real era of South African posters began in the 1980s with the formation of the Screen Training Project (STP) in Johannesburg, and the Community Arts Project (CAP) Media Project in Cape Town.

Posters from exile

Posters supporting the liberation struggle in South Africa have been produced throughout the world to raise international awareness of the inequities of apartheid. But in 1978, just across the border from South Africa, a group of exiled South African cultural workers began to print posters with a different purpose.

3 c1941. Anti-fascist, pro-Allied poster produced to raise funds in South Africa for the Soviet war effort in the 1940s. *Source: South African Library, Cape Town*

Medu Art Ensemble was formed in Botswana to use art to give voice to the growing struggle of the people 'at home'. Medu designed posters for distribution inside South Africa, to be used by organisations directly confronting the apartheid state. Medu called for the South African mass movement to develop silkscreening as a communications technique. Silkscreening, they said, requires relatively little equipment or capital outlay, does not need electricity, and the skills can be easily taught.

In July 1982, over 5 000 cultural workers from South Africa participated in the Medu-organised Culture and Resistance Festival in Gaborone. They carried back with them the conference theme: *political struggle is an unavoidable part of life in South Africa, and it must therefore infuse our art and culture.*

After the conference, the South African state banned Medu posters within days of publication. Distribution crumbled as people risked years in jail for smuggling posters across the border.

At the same time, activists had formed silk-screen workshops in South Africa which produced and distributed posters far more effectively in response to immediate demands. Medu was no longer needed in the same way.

At 1am on 14 June 1985, South African army units crossed the border and attacked Gaborone, killing 12 people. Among the dead were leading graphic artist and Medu official Thami Mnyele, and Medu treasurer Mike Hamlyn. The homes of several other Medu artists were destroyed. Remaining South African members of Medu left Botswana, or went underground. Medu ceased to exist.

4 1950s. The combined strength of all freedom-loving South Africans is more than a match for Hendrick Verwoerd, the father of apartheid, and his government.
Source: IDAF Photographic Library

Silkscreening in Johannesburg

In 1979 the Johannesburg-based Junction Avenue community of cultural workers silkscreened posters for the Fattis and Monis pasta boycott, supporting workers dismissed during a strike. The group went on to make posters for other worker struggles, including the red meat strike in 1980 and the Wilson-Rowntree sweet boycott of 1981. Also in 1981, a community-based labour support structure, Rock Against Management (RAM), commissioned artists to produce posters challenging the proposed celebration of 20 years of South Africa as a republic under a white minority government.

Out of this activity, a part-time voluntary workshop was born, providing in-house training, printing posters and T-shirts, and offering training to community organisations. Their first poster attacked the imminent 'independence' of the Ciskei, one of the apartheid-created African 'homelands'.

In 1983, the UDF amalgamated over 600 grassroots and civic organisations into a national anti-apartheid body. The Front backed a proposal that the part-time workshop become a full-time facility serving all UDF affiliates. In November 1983, the Screen Training Project came into being.

STP aimed to train members of community organisations in silkscreening techniques, to help set up workshops around the country, and to provide production facilities for organisations to produce their own media on STP's premises.

Soon a steady stream of activists from all over the Transvaal, the Orange Free State, and parts of the Cape was passing through the workshop, producing thousands of posters, T-shirts, badges and banners. The demand stretched the project's resources – human and technical – to the limit.

The quality of posters produced in the workshops was often atrocious. Hand-lettered and hand-painted stencils, and printing carried out at breakneck speed by absolute beginners, led to all kinds of streaking and blotching.

But there were sound reasons why the demand remained. Silkscreening allowed for full participation by the newly recruited membership of UDF organisations, involving up to 20 people at a time in preparation and printing. The process permitted short 'runs' at relatively low cost, which proved perfect for publicising hundreds of local meetings and activities.

The new project also attracted unwanted, but not unexpected, attention from other quarters. After only six months of operating, STP workers arrived at the workshop to find the gates forced open, furniture and screening equipment wrecked, and the project's brand-new photocopier smashed. The vandals were never traced.

5 1958. The ANC continued its 1952 Defiance Campaign into the late 1950s with this call for a stayaway – the £1-a-day campaign was a demand raised by SACTU.
Source: Baily's Photo Archives, Johannesburg

In 1984, security police arrived at the project's new premises and confiscated a large number of posters. In the same period, the state banned a T-shirt produced at the workshop by activists from the Eastern Cape.

At the start of the first State of Emergency in 1985, a worker from STP was detained for four months. No reasons were given. In 1986, on the first day of the second Emergency, police waited at the door of STP from 4am. But project staff were expecting this new crackdown, and had gone into hiding.

However, the same worker was detained two months later. The police claimed that he was *'the co-ordinator of the so-called screen programme, an organisation responsible for the printing and distribution of subversive literature in the Johan-*

6 1977. After the 1976 uprising, a bill was passed extending the powers of the police and protecing them from prosecution for acts carried out during the uprising, even if such actions were illegal.
Source: Projects Committee Library, Wits University

WHO FOOTS THE BILL?

nesburg area, and also actively involved in the training of Black Youths of the Soweto Youth Congress and the Alexandra Youth Congress.' Five more STP workers were detained over the next few months.

These acts of repression forced STP underground. The project found secret offices, and could not advertise its services to the community. Although STP was set up primarily as a training workshop, staff were so tied up in production that the training component was neglected. Community organisations remained unable to produce posters without the assistance of STP staff. With STP in hiding, silkscreen production declined.

STP re-emerged as the Media Training Workshop (MTW) after the unbannings of 1990, but with the disbanding of the UDF in 1991 the project's future remains uncertain.

Printing in Cape Town

In the wave of interest generated by the Culture and Resistance Festival in Botswana in mid-1982, a group of cultural workers resolved to establish a screen-printing resource centre based at the Community Arts Project in Cape Town.

A year later, a simple workshop was equipped – with a printing table, drying lines, a bathtub, an exposure box and a huge vertical camera dis-

BIKO AND SOLIDARITY

BLACK PEOPLE'S CONVENTION TRIBUTE TO THE LATE HONORARY PRESIDENT BANTU STEPHEN BIKO
One Azania: One Nation

7 1977. The death in detention of Black Consciousness leader, Steve Biko, sent shock-waves around the world.
Source: South African History Archives, Johannesburg

carded by a printing company. Although a few posters were produced – the CAYCO launch poster, and posters for a few CAP events – the workshop was hardly used.

At this point, a few members of the original group introduced a series of weekend workshops for community organisations, unions and educational projects. They invited all progressive organisations to make their posters with CAP's assistance.

The slow trickle of users became a flood with the launch of the UDF. By late 1983, the workshop was in use day and night. A used screen left the printing table only to be replaced by the next in line; posters were force-dried with hair-driers for instant distribution; and the floor of the wash-out room was constantly flooded.

The south-easter gusting through the workshop every time the door opened only made matters worse, gluing wet posters together as they hung on the drying lines, and covering everything with sand. Frequent outbreaks of hilarity may have owed something to the heavy fog of ink and thinners.

This was only the start of an almost uninterrupted flow of work – bannings, restrictions and States of Emergency notwithstanding. When organisations could no longer hold public meetings, they organised fun-runs, cultural evenings, fetes and snack-dances – these needed posters too.

The workshop also printed stickers, buttons and T-shirts. T-shirts in particular became so widespread as 'walking posters' that CAP created a separate facility to produce them. (The state felt obliged to counter the popularity of such T-shirts and passed a short-lived law banning them.) The workshop evolved further to incorporate banner-making and, to a lesser degree, fabric-printing.

But CAP, like STP in Johannesburg, encountered problems. Daily requests for short workshops, technical assistance, and use of the facilities, swamped long-term training objectives.

Both STP and CAP found that training programmes had to be tailored to 'fit the case' in every situation, taking into account language, local conditions, schooling, political experience, technical experience, and many other disparate factors. 'Blueprints' for training were useless.

Further, training must be backed up by access to resources, and should meet the organisation's needs. Newly acquired skills, if not practised, are quickly lost. Both projects found that they trained fewer people more slowly than initially anticipated.

Unlike STP, CAP was not forced to go underground. It was subjected to a degree of harassment, but continued operating openly. Unfortunately, like so many other anti-apartheid service structures, CAP has found itself starved of resources in the new political climate following the unbannings of 1990. Its future, therefore, is also not certain.

8 1981. The 20th anniversary of South Africa's white minority Republic was marked by massive protest action around the country.
Source: Private collection, Johannesburg

Posters in Natal

While posters were produced in Natal, there was no central poster workshop similar to CAP or STP. After the formation of the UDF, a broad media grouping was set up which was linked to the community newspaper *Ukusa*. Fine arts students working with this grouping helped design posters; some were commercially printed, but most were silkscreened at the University of Durban-Westville (UDW).

The UDW Students' Representative Council, working with fine arts students, also set up small silkscreen workshops in the community, primarily in the Indian areas of Chatsworth and Merebank.

Posters silkscreened at the University of Natal, Durban, were mainly for student organisations such as COSAS, AZASO and NUSAS.

In 1987, the United Committee of Concern started a workshop in Wentworth, Durban, to service organisations in coloured areas. Their work also extended to other UDF structures. They produced media for FAWU's 'Boycott Clover' campaign, and 'Don't vote' posters for the campaign against community council elections in black townships.

The Natal UDF set up its own media workshop under conditions of extreme secrecy. The workshop designed its own material and reproduced leaflets and publications from national structures. Enterprising members of local civic structures organised metalworkers in the community to make proper silkscreens for the workshop to use.

Some organisations relied largely on professional photoscreening services. As violence escalated and with almost weekly funerals of activists, commemorative T-shirts and posters were produced using this service. The advantage it offered was photoscreening, essential to the reproduction of photographs of the deceased. Photoscreening technology was available to the Mass Democratic Movement, but was never used widely, largely because it became possible at the same time as desk-top publishing (DTP) replaced silkscreening as a major means of poster production.

The advent of DTP and laser printers made typeset posters accessible to many organisations. The Media Resource Centre at the University of Natal, Durban, the Resource Centre at the Ecumenical Centre in town, the SRCs of UND and UDW and some service organisations became places where poster designs could be produced quickly and easily, with relatively good security. Prior to this, typesetting in Durban was done through a commercial newspaper. Security was always a problem, and many organisations did not have the skills to use the equipment.

While organisations were able to produce more posters this way, disadvantages included the cost of having posters printed instead of silkscreened, the unimaginative designs produced by people new to computers and DTP, and the loss of the organisational benefits of many people together producing media.

The Durban Democratic Association (a UDF affiliate in central Durban) developed an imaginative solution. They printed black and white typeset posters, and then involved members of the organisation in spraypainting other colours onto the posters (by 1989, usually green and yellow).

9 1981. In 1981 the Ciskei became the second of the bantustans to accept Pretoria's so-called independence, though not without a fight from organisations throughout South Africa.
Source: South African History Archive, Johannesburg

The problem of bad design has meant that posters and other media are often taken to progressive specialists who produce good designs at lower than commercial rates for organisations. While this produced better media in the late 1980s, it meant skills have been even further removed from grassroots activists.

The Durban Media Trainers' Group, a continuation of the earlier Durban Media Workshop, was formed in 1988 to organise media skills training in Durban and surrounding areas. It has offered training in computer literacy, DTP, silkscreening and poster design. Courses have been run for over 50 community, environmental, welfare, political, church and student organisations. The training emphasised media as an organisational tool, the aim being to empower organisations in the planning, design and production of effective posters using a variety of methods. This has gone some way to addressing the problem of overcentralised skills. Training has been taken to informal settlements and low-tech groups as well as urban-based organisations.

COSATU

CAP, STP and other silkscreen workshops produced posters for trade union struggles in the early 1980s. But the launch of the Congress of South African Trade Unions (COSATU) in 1985 led to a different kind of demand for posters.

As a national trade union organisation, COSATU needed not a few hundred posters for each local event, but thousands and even tens of thousands of copies, usually in two or three colours (red, yellow and black being COSATU's colours). Offset litho printing was the only real option.

This was not new: some UDF national posters had been commercially printed. But under the Emergency, commercial printers risked serious trouble taking on UDF jobs, including prosecution under the Publications Act. The state appeared initially hesitant to use blatant repressive tactics against trade unions, and COSATU was able to employ commercial printers for very large print-runs.

In May 1987, COSATU acquired its own press in Johannesburg. It printed one colour of its first print-run of 10 000 copies. Before the second colour could be printed, 'persons unknown' bombed COSATU House, destroying the building and completely demolishing the brand-new press.

10 1982. The Culture and Resistance Festival in Botswana was a turning point for South African postermaking. *Source: Private collection, Johannesburg*

COSATU resorted once again to printing posters commercially. Of course they still faced problems. Posters always seemed to be needed for today and yesterday. Sympathetic printers produced posters overnight, risking intensified state harassment. After posters were printed, workers sticking them up in the streets often had trouble with police.

Despite differences in scale and production, COSATU posters are part of the same tradition as those from the silkscreen workshops. As the federation grows into the post-apartheid era, posters will continue to play an important part in mobilising and educating their members.

Other poster producers

The Media and Resource Services (MARS) project produced two types of posters between 1983 and 1985.

Staff at this Johannesburg-based community media centre designed A2-size colour posters for major groupings which wanted 'professional' posters and could pay printers to reproduce between

11 1982. One of the first posters produced at CAP. *Source: Community Arts Project, Cape Town*

2 000 and 5 000 copies. Once users approved the design and slogans, MARS organised the offset litho printing. Some of these bright and innovative posters included those for the UDF's Signature Campaign and People's Music Festival, and the poster for the first Free Mandela rally held by the Release Mandela Campaign in Soweto 1984.

MARS also produced A3-size black and white photocopied posters, to meet the urgent demands of smaller events, such as those held by the various youth congresses. For example, a COSAS branch in Mamelodi would need 50 posters to publicise a meeting. MARS staff would provide on the job training in letraset and design, and assist users with typesetting if desired. Many groups came to MARS to produce pamphlets and newsletters, which they often enlarged to A3 format for wall or office display.

MARS was also a victim of state repression and was forced to close down during the second State of Emergency.

The Graphic Equalizer was a privately-owned design and reprographic studio started with funding from Ravan Press. Faced with a frequently hostile commercial printing industry, many democratic organisations and alternative media turned to the Graphic Equalizer. Throughout the turbulent 1980s, the Equalizer trained groups in the technical skills needed to produce the printed word. For two years, it ran a successful project for school leavers, teaching the skills needed to design and produce posters. The Graphic Equalizer closed down in 1989.

The Other Press Service (TOPS) also engaged in postermaking and skills training. Formed by three journalists in 1987, TOPS' initial work was restricted to the design and production of newsletters and pamphlets, mainly for trade unions and youth congresses.

In late 1987 the organisation acquired its own DTP equipment, and TOPS began to assist in graphic production.

With a full-time staff of three, TOPS now runs a service structure, which typesets, designs and produces media for organisations ranging from rural youth congresses to the head offices of the ANC, SACP and COSATU. They provide an in-house training course for media activists, with special emphasis on DTP, and conduct media training workshops throughout the region. They advise organisations and publications on how to develop their own media strategy.

Choosing images

Like any other work of art, a poster represents a set of aesthetic choices about image, colour, technique and style. These choices are made within a framework defined by existing materials, technical skills, and the ideology of the people and organisations making the choices. In spite of the differences in reproductive processes used by the groups involved, their diverse backgrounds and the large distances between them, such choices and limitations contributed to the similarities of style which characterise the posters of this period.

The first common denominator lies in the imagery, which centres on a relatively small range of political symbols. Some reflect an international visual vocabulary of struggle, such as clenched fists and banners, drawing a link between the issues confronting people in all societies of the world. These images were not only repeated, but also reinterpreted, redrawn and redesigned in ways specific to, and often personally felt by, the people producing them.

Other symbols are unique to South Africa, such as the spear and shield of the ANC and MK, or the photograph of the dying Hector Peterson.

Colour is also symbolic: black, green, and gold for the ANC, red, yellow and black for the UDF and COSATU, and red for struggle, socialism and the SACP.

Apartheid has left South African communities with a limited common vocabulary of images. Colonial suppression of popular culture left little unifying national 'folk' imagery to draw on, such as might be found in the traditional costume of Chile, or the rich connotations of the 'life-force' represented by the skeleton in Mexico. Traditional symbols that survive have often been trivialised and distorted to fit apartheid's ethnic categories.

Therefore almost every symbol of resistance or political demand had to be established through on-the-ground organisational activity. Each repetition of an image drove it deeper into the cultural awareness of the community. Fists and flags became 'our fists' and 'our flags'. The image of Hector Peterson, the pictures of marching crowds and waving banners became, in some deeper sense, our own.

People increasingly drew images from observing the reality of struggle around them. Time passed and fresh images were incorporated: the tanks and casspirs of the police and army occupation of the townships; the AK-47; the tin shacks of squatter camps; and the clothing, faces and gestures of militant youth and workers. At the end of the decade, portraits of ANC and SACP leaders burst onto the scene, together with the resurgent colours and symbols of the organisations.

Although there is no doubting its effectiveness, such repetition of imagery has at times been a problem. Some media workers feel resistance culture should aim higher than simply popularising key symbols, scenes and personalities. Should postermakers, they ask, confront the issues of cultural creativity – provoking critical thought, challenging precepts, breaking the rules of aesthetic convention – in short, fostering cultural awareness as well as mobilising people politically? These questions must still be answered. Yet, whatever the merits of the aesthetic debate, there can be no doubt that these posters represent, in an important and powerful way, the voices of people previously silent.

A second common feature of most posters of this period is production technique. Many have a hand-made or unskilled appearance, using silk-screen technology in its cheapest and simplest form, hand-drawn images and text, hand-cut or painted stencils, and 'line photography' where photographs were used.

This is partly the result of a lack of resources. But the choice was also motivated by other considerations. The few skilled artists who identified with the people's movement believed they should encourage people to develop their own imagery. Technically skilled workers who supervised the workshops insisted that user groups themselves pick up a squeegee and print the posters they would be using in their communities. These two strands – of political imagery on the one hand, and a community-oriented technology on the other – were the dominant influences on the thousands of posters produced during the 1980s. Other aesthetic influences, however, can also be traced.

Those few trained artists who brought their skills to the poster workshops did so out of political conviction. Visual imagery of struggle and revolution from other parts of the world often influenced them directly – posters and images from the Russian revolution, from Germany in the 1930s, from France and the US in the 1960s, from Cuba, Nicaragua and Chile, and from the murals and posters of Mozambique in the 1970s. A strong parallel influence came from contemporary black South African artists, drawing on the black consciousness movement of the 1970s, and on the African aesthetic tradition of expressionistic distortion and economy of line and shape.

But these artistic influences should not be over-emphasised. The heart of the process lay in the engagement between those who used the workshops, for whom media production had become a necessary element of political life, and those who ran the workshops, whose central concern lay in democratising visual communications.

In sum, these posters represent a major form of popular visual expression of the period, if not the major form. They are built upon the perceptions, realities and demands of the communities which produced them. People who had been deprived of visual expression turned their hands and creative impulses to making these posters. Many are exciting and beautiful to look at; others show the effects of being a 'first effort' battle with techniques. But above all, they map the spirit of the period – a people's struggle against repression, but also their struggle to catch and reflect a glimpse of a future democratic society.

The next decade and further ...

Two aspects stand out from the uneven development of a poster tradition in South Africa.

Firstly, there is an abundance of enthusiasm, ability and potential for small-scale, grassroots media production. That much is evident in the pages of this book. Secondly, the tools for this kind of communication should be made available to the widest possible audience.

Over the last few years, media production within the progressive movement has tended to become more centralised. Organisations depend on computer-generated type and design for the sake of speed, convenience, and 'professional' appearance. Posters have tended to become uniform, mechanically functional in appearance, and all too often with lines of Helvetica in varying sizes.

Most posters are now printed commercially. This makes sense for the central structures of organisations like COSATU and the ANC, which have to produce large numbers of posters quickly. But smaller organisations cannot afford commercial production, and have often stopped using posters. High technology production also concentrates skills in just a few hands.

Silkscreening and other simple, non-mechanised forms of design and production make it possible to involve even the most technically inexperienced in the most far-flung communities in writing, drawing, designing and producing their own media. The low cost of the equipment and of the printing method also bring printing within economic reach for most communities.

12 1984. Silkscreening at a community workshop.
Source: South African History Archive, Johannesburg

CAP and STP were the 'barefoot' element in the development of the media as the voice of people's power over the past decade. This element must continue in a future South Africa.

The democratic movement faces a daunting number of media challenges over the next period. The greatest is finding a place in the mainstream mass media. If mainstream media is to speak to, and for, the people of South Africa, it must be informed and stimulated by its living counterpart at grassroots level. This process cannot be taken for granted, nor is it a romantic vision. There must be serious thought and necessary resources to ensure that a popular voice continues to be heard.

We look forward to moving away from the confrontation and destruction which marked the years of struggle against apartheid. The process of building a just and democratic South Africa demands that all the people of our diverse communities participate in reconstruction. Posters can play a key role in that process: educating and informing people, promoting literacy programmes, health and safety campaigns, and recruiting support for other social projects.

At the same time, posters can also provide a vehicle for activists and grassroots members to contribute their own ideas to this reconstruction. Posters can carry not only the word of the state to the people, but the voice of the people themselves.

Over the decade of the 1980s, posters in South Africa played a crucial role in expressing the demands and beliefs of communities suffering under apartheid. Now, in the 1990s, we should use posters in the key task of building a national consciousness among all South Africans. In so doing, South Africa could take the art and practise of postermaking to new heights. ❏

Images from exile

A selection of posters from Medu Art Ensemble, Botswana

'What does true political conciousness mean to the artist in my country? We need to clearly popularise and give dignity to the just thoughts and deeds of the people. . . It was in Medu Art Ensemble where the role of an artist concretised itself: the role of an artist is to learn; the role of an artist is to teach others; the role of an artist is to ceaselessly search for the ways and means of achieving freedom. Art cannot overthrow a government, but it can inspire change.'
Thami Mnyele, Culture and Resistance Festival, Gaborone, 1982.

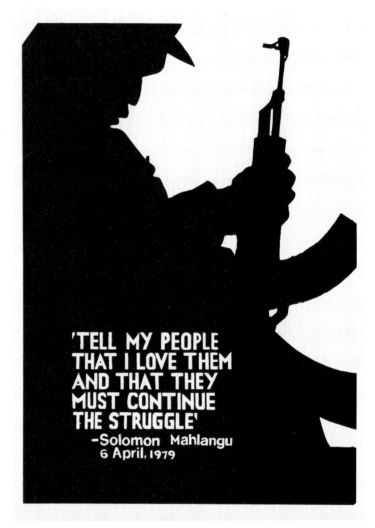

'TELL MY PEOPLE THAT I LOVE THEM AND THAT THEY MUST CONTINUE THE STRUGGLE'
—Solomon Mahlangu
6 April, 1979

13 1982. Commemoration of the execution of MK member Solomon Mahlangu.
Silkscreened poster produced by Medu for the ANC
Black

LET US ALL SUPPORT THE FIGHT!

NO TO RESETTLEMENT!

14 1981. Poster protesting continuing removals.
Silkscreened poster produced by Medu
Black and red

15 1981. 9 August, South African Women's Day; the wording comes from the song sung on the 9 August 1956 women's march on Pretoria.
Silkscreened poster produced by Medu, Black marbled with green and yellow

16 1983. 16 December, Hero's Day (poster drawn by Thami Mnyele, killed by SADF soldiers in a cross-border raid in 1985).
Offset litho poster produced by Medu Black and red

17 1982. 26 June, South African Freedom Day (marking the adoption of the Freedom Charter by the Congress of the People in 1955).
Silk-screened poster produced by Medu Black marbled with red

Forward to people's power!

Politics

Forward to people's power!

The struggle for democracy and non-racialism in South Africa has been a long one. For more than 300 years, since the arrival of the first colonialists, South Africans fought in various ways against the theft of their land, racial oppression and economic exploitation. But it is the 1980s which will go down in history as the decade of mass organisation. By the last days of 1989, this organisation had become so resilient and strong it was clear that the decisive shift from the politics of resistance to the politics of transformation was about to take place.

Strands of resistance

The British colonial authorities handed power to the white settlers of South Africa in 1910. On the 8 January 1912, the African National Congress (ANC) was founded (under its original name of the South African National Native Congress). The ANC aimed to unite all existing black organisations working for a non-racial society into one strong force.

A second organisation, the Communist Party of South Africa (now called the South African Communist Party, SACP) was founded in 1921. Although initially located among white workers, the party soon turned its efforts to mobilising the much larger black working class, linking the struggle against economic exploitation with the fight against national oppression.

Over time, the ANC and the SACP, together with the nascent black trade unions, formed a close working relationship in the struggle for a national democracy.

In 1948, the National Party was voted into power. Their first priority was to stem the tide of resistance to segregation and racial discrimination. In 1950, the Suppression of Communism Act was passed, effectively banning the Communist Party. The Act also cast a wider net – it was phrased in such a way as to allow the state to brand as communist anyone who attempted to change the prevailing political situation. The National Party also moved rapidly to introduce apartheid, a legally-enforced policy of racial segregation and discrimination.

But while the 1950s entrenched racial segregation in South Africa, that decade also marked the beginning of intense and sustained popular defiance to institutionalised racism. The ANC Youth League, under Nelson Mandela and Oliver Tambo, began the first Defiance Campaign, involving thousands in mass refusals to obey the new apartheid laws. This momentum led to the Congress of the People: on 26 June 1955 delegates from all over the country put forward the demands in the document known as the Freedom Charter.

The government could not permit this militancy. On 21 March 1960 police opened fire on a peaceful crowd in Sharpeville, killing 69 people. When the ANC called for a national stayaway to protest this massacre, the government banned both the ANC and the Pan Africanist Congress (PAC) (formed by elements that broke away from the ANC in 1959). The ANC turned to a long 30 years of underground work.

The 1960s also marked the beginning of the armed struggle. After so many decades of peaceful resistance in the face of state violence, the ANC concluded that force must be met with force, and formed its military wing Umkhonto we Sizwe (MK), the Spear of the Nation.

In October 1963, leaders of the ANC and MK were arrested at Lilliesleaf farm in Rivonia near Johannesburg. When they were finally brought to trial, Nelson Mandela, already serving a sentence for leaving the country illegally, was charged along with them. Eight of the accused were sentenced to life imprisonment.

During the late 1960s and early 1970s the apartheid government appeared to have finally enforced an unwilling quiesence. The ANC, SACP and PAC were banned. MK continued its preparations for a sabotage campaign, but mass protests were muted. The emergence of black trade unionism in 1973, and of black student protest, seemed but a minor crack in the facade. That apparent passivity ended on 16 June 1976. Police opened fire on youths protesting apartheid education; within days, an uprising spread throughout the black South African townships. In the months that followed, thousands of protesters were killed by the police, others were jailed, and still others left the country to join the ANC, MK and other exiled organisations. As time went by, the anger and militancy were transformed into organised mass political protest.

The people re-organise

The mass movement of the 1980s brought together a number of political and organisational strands. Building on the militancy of the 1976 youth uprising, it revived the vision of a united non-racial democratic South Africa embodied in the Freedom Charter. The demands of the Freedom Charter gave ideological direction and organisational unity to the spontaneous anger generated by the repression that followed 1976.

This focus on the Freedom Charter also renewed mass interest in the Congress movement, led by the ANC, then entering its third decade as a banned organisation. Meanwhile, the state tried a reformist strategy, introducing a new constitution that created coloured and Indian chambers in the South African parliament, but still excluded Africans from central political participation and firmly retained white control.

The mass movement responded by forming the United Democratic Front in August 1983. The UDF brought together more than 600 youth structures, student organisations, trade unions, church groups, civic organisations, women's groups and political organisations. It identified clearly with the ANC and the Congress tradition. Old Congress structures like the Transvaal Indian Congress, which was never banned, joined the UDF along with new organisations which emerged for the first time in the 1980s. The UDF umbrella gave these groups a political focus directed at central state power, and also an organisational capacity and impact far beyond the individual potential of each structure.

This capacity was demonstrated in the campaign to reject the tri-cameral parliament and the black local authorities structure. Using slogans such as 'Votes For All', and through boycotts of elections for the tri-cameral parliament and black local authorities, the UDF convincingly demonstrated the determination of South Africa's people to fight token solutions, and to demand access to real political power.

Mass organisation – civics, youth and women's structures – developed fast. Non-violent forms of political protest mushroomed: boycotts, stayaways, demonstrations and marches backed up demands connected with local issues such as rent increases, education and health problems, corruption in local authorities and transport shortages. The UDF convincingly linked these local grassroots issues to broader national political demands.

In September 1984, a year after the founding of the UDF, police fired on a protest march in Sebokeng. The townships erupted again. The people turned on those they viewed as state puppets, such as community councillors, township administrators and the police: their houses were burned, they were killed or had to flee. Army troops were sent in to quell the uprising, but they used a level of violence that simply re-fuelled people's anger. Both the ANC underground and the legal structures of the UDF worked to give form to this outburst. Tactics like consumer boycotts and mass stayaways were wielded with immense power. Many of the discredited black local authorities collapsed.

The state crackdown

In July 1985, the state declared a partial State of Emergency, banning all public meetings, arresting and detaining activists, and sending troops to occupy townships. But while repression disrupted the activities of national organisations, it also forced the process of mass mobilisation to become local and decentralised. New organisational structures, such as street, zone and block committees sprang up in the townships. These structures brought a new rallying call for people's power – empowerment of all the people from the street level up.

The state imposed successive States of Emergency. Although increasingly forced underground, activists replied with ongoing political campaigns – against the bantustan system, the tri-cameral parliament and black local authorities, against continuing repression and economic exploitation, for the unbanning of organisations, for votes for all in a united South Africa. The Emergency wrought havoc on the economy and tightened the noose of international disapproval. South Africa's isolation became almost complete. In the face of this, the white monolith began to crack, and the first of a series of influential whites made their way to Lusaka to meet with the ANC and discover what this illegal but ever-present force had to say about the future.

By early 1989, the Mass Democratic Movement (a general term used to identify the organisations which could not organise openly under the State of Emergency) called for a second Defiance Campaign to demand that troops leave the townships, an end to the Emergency, and the unbanning of popular opposition organisations. At the heart of this campaign lay the call to unban the ANC.

As the decade drew to a close, it was clear to all, including the apartheid government, that without the ANC there would be no solution to South Africa's problems.

On 2 February 1990, the regime unbanned the ANC, the SACP and the PAC. Nine days later, on 11 February 1990, Nelson Rolihlahla Mandela was freed after 27 years in prison.

The ten fighting years of the 1980s had brought the South African people closer to freedom than ever before. ❑

CONGRESS

ocratic South Africa

18 1990. One of the first ANC posters produced inside South Africa since the unbanning of the organisation on 2 February 1990 – it popularises the ANC's slogan for the year.
Offset litho poster produced by the Media Committee of the NRC, Johannesburg Full colour

UDF DEMANDS UNBAN THE ANC

19 1986. The UDF calls for the unbanning of the ANC.
Offset litho poster produced by the UDF, Johannesburg
Black

We the youth

We congratulate Comrade Tambo on the occasion of his 70th birthday. We wish him many more years as a leader on the road to freedom and to the building of a liberated South Africa.

TIME-TESTED LEADER OF THE PEOPLE OF SOUTH AFRICA

- Born 27th October 1917
- Joined the struggle in 1944
- Has been peoples leader since 1969
- Wishing you many more birthdays

FREE MANDELA! MASS RALLY

REGINA MUNDI
SUNDAY SEPTEMBER 4
The people shall govern

20 1987. SAYCO celebrates the 70th birthday of Oliver Tambo, then exiled president of the ANC.
Offset litho poster produced for SAYCO by Graphic Equalizer, Johannesburg
Black, red, yellow and green

21 1984. The RMC regularly called for the freeing of Nelson Mandela and other political prisoners in the 1980s.
Offset litho poster produced by RMC, Johannesburg
Black, green and yellow

22 1986. The UDF celebrates the anniversary of the 1955 adoption of the Freedom Charter at the Congress of the People, and calls for the unbanning of the ANC.
Offset litho poster produced by STP for the UDF, Johannesburg
Black, green and yellow

24 1989. Celebrating the release of Walter Sisulu and other ANC leaders from prison in October 1989.
Offset litho poster issued by the NRC, Johannesburg
Black, green and yellow

MPETHA KATHRADA MLANGENI

MOTSOALEDI MKWAYI MHLABA

SISULU

LONG LIVE THE ANC!

25 1989. On the release of Walter Sisulu and other Rivonia trialists in October 1989.
Offset litho poster produced by TOPS for the NRC, Johannesburg
Black, green and yellow

23 1987. This 'instant' mural celebrating the release of ANC leader Govan Mbeki from life imprisonment is made up of six A1 size posters used together.
Silkscreened poster produced at CAP by the Gardens Media Group for the Welcome Mbeki Committee, Cape Town
Black, green and yellow

26 1989. Legal protest marches took place for the first time in years in 1989 – this poster was carried by thousands of people at a Johannesburg march (the ANC was still banned).
Offset litho poster produced for the NRC by TOPS, Johannesburg
Black

27 1989. The ANC continued to exert its leadership role over the years, even while it was banned.
Offset litho poster produced by Learn and Teach, Johannesburg
Black, green and yellow

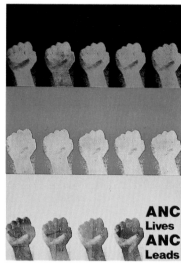

28 1989. This portrait was painted from verbal descriptions by people who had visited Mandela in prison, as it is illegal to publish the photograph of a prisoner.
Offset litho poster produced by COSATU, Johannesburg
Full colour

29 1990. After being banned in 1950, and operating underground until 2 February 1990, the SACP is relaunched on the anniversary of the formation of the CPSA in 1921.
Offset litho poster produced for the SACP, Johannesburg Black, red and yellow

30 1990. A history of the Communist Party in South Africa since its inception in 1921.
Offset litho poster produced by TOPS for the SACP, Johannesburg Black, red and yellow

WE, THE PEOPLE of South Africa, declare for all our country and the world to know:
That South Africa belongs to all who live in it, black and white, and that no government can justly claim authority unless it is based on the will of the people;
That our people have been robbed of their birthright to land, liberty and peace by a form of government founded on injustice and inequality;
That our country will never be prosperous or free until all our people live in brotherhood, enjoying equal rights and opportunities;
That only a democratic state, based on the will of the people can secure to all their birthright without distinction of colour, race, sex or belief;
And therefore, we the people of South Africa, black and white, together equals, countrymen and brothers adopt this FREEDOM CHARTER. And we pledge ourselves to strive together, sparing nothing of our strength and courage, until the democratic changes here set out have been won.

The People Shall Govern

Every man and woman shall have the right to vote for and stand as a candidate for all bodies which make laws;
All the people shall be entitled to take part in the administration of the country;
The rights of the people shall be the same regardless of race, colour or sex;
All bodies of minority rule, advisory boards, councils and authorities shall be replaced by democratic organs of self-government.

All National Groups Shall Have Equal Rights!

There shall be equal status in the bodies of state, in the courts and in the schools for all national groups and races;
All national groups shall be protected by law against insults to their race and national pride;
All people shall have equal rights to use their own language and to develop their own folk culture and customs;
The preaching and practice of national, race or colour discrimination and contempt shall be a punishable crime;
All apartheid laws and practices shall be set aside.

The People Shall Share In The Country's Wealth!

The national wealth of our country, the heritage of all South Africans, shall be restored to the people;
The mineral wealth beneath the soil, the banks and monopoly industry shall be transferred to the ownership of the people as a whole;
All other industries and trade shall be controlled to assist the well-being of the people;
All shall have equal rights to trade where they choose, to manufacture and to enter all trades, crafts and professions

The Land Shall Be Shared Among Those Who Work It!

Restriction of land ownership on a racial basis shall be ended, and all the land re-divided amongst those who work it, to banish famine and land hunger;
The state shall help the peasants with implements, seed, tractors and dams to save the soil and assist the tillers;
Freedom of movement shall be guaranteed to all who work on the land;
All shall have the right to occupy land wherever they choose;
People shall not be robbed of their cattle, and forced labour and farm prisons shall be abolished.

All Shall Be Equal Before The Law!

No one shall be imprisoned, deported or restricted without fair trial;
No one shall be condemned by the order of any Government official;
The courts shall be representative of all the people;
Imprisonment shall be only for serious crimes against the people, and shall aim at re-education, not vengeance;
The police force and army shall be open to all on an equal basis and shall be the helpers and protectors of the people;
All laws which discriminate on the grounds of race, colour or belief shall be repealed.

COSA SALU 32 YE OF T FREE CHAR

*Friday, 26 June, 1987 is the 32nd anni Freedom Charter by the Congress of th
*The Freedom Charter is supported by Africa and is widely regarded as the m from our liberation struggle.
*The Freedom Charter is supported by represent over half the total membersh by hundreds and thousands of other wo

COSATU WORKERS - Make sure there discussion of the Charter and its mean a worker-controlled society free of op

All Shall Enjoy Hun

The law shall guarantee to all their right to speak, to o to worship and to educate their children;

The privacy of the house from police raids shall be protected by law;
All shall be free to travel without restriction from countryside to town, from province to province, and from South Africa abroad.
Pass laws, permits and all other laws restricting these freedoms shall be abolished.

There Shall Be Work And Security!

All who work shall be free to form trade unions, to elect their officers and to make wage agreements with their employers;
The state shall recognise the right and duty of all to work, and to draw full unemployment benefits;
Men and women of all races shall receive equal pay for equal work;
There shall be a forty-hour working week, a national minimum wage, paid annual leave, and sick leave for all workers, and maternity leave on full pay for all working mothers;
Miners, domestic workers, farm workers and civil servants shall have the same rights as all others who work;
Child labour, compound labour, the tot system and contract labour shall be abolished.

The Doors Of Learning And Culture Shall Be Opened!

The government shall discover, develop and encourage national talent for the enhancement of our cultural life;
All the cultural treasures of mankind shall be open to all, by free exchange of books, ideas and contact with other lands;
The aim of education shall be to teach the youth to love their people and their culture, to honour human brotherhood, liberty and peace;
Education shall be free, compulsory, universal and equal for all children;
Higher education and technical training shall be opened to all by means of state allowances and scholarships awarded on the basis of merit;
Adult illiteracy shall be ended by a mass state education plan;
Teachers shall have all the rights of other citizens;
The colour bar in cultural life, in sport and in education shall be abolished.

There Shall Be Houses, Security And Comfort!

All people shall have the right to live where they choose, to be decently housed, and to bring up their families in comfort and security;
Unused housing space to be made available to the people;
Rent and prices shall be lowered, food plentiful and no one shall go hungry;
A preventive health scheme shall be run by the state;
Free medical care and hospitalisation shall be provided for all, with special care for mothers and young children;
Slums shall be demolished and new suburbs built where all shall have transport, roads, lighting, playing fields, creches and social centres;
The aged, the orphans, the disabled and the sick shall be cared for by the state;
Rest, leisure and recreation shall be the right of all;
Fenced locations and ghettoes shall be abolished and laws which break up families shall be repealed.

There Shall Be Peace And Friendship!

South Africa shall be a fully independent state, which respects the rights and sovereignty of all nations;
South Africa shall strive to maintain world peace and the settlement of all international disputes by negotiation not war;
Peace and friendship amongst all our people shall be secured by upholding the equal rights, opportunities and status of all;
The people of the protectorates Basutoland, Bechuanaland and Swaziland shall be free to decide for themselves their own future;
The right of all the peoples of Africa to independence and self-government shall be recognised, and shall be the basis of close cooperation.

Let all who love their people and their country now say, as we say here:
THESE FREEDOMS WE WILL FIGHT FOR, SIDE BY SIDE, THROUGHOUT OUR LIVES UNTIL WE HAVE WON OUR LIBERTY.

31 1987. COSATU pays tribute to the Congress of the People and adoption of the Freedom Charter on 26 June 1955. *Offset litho poster issued by COSATU, Johannesburg Black and yellow*

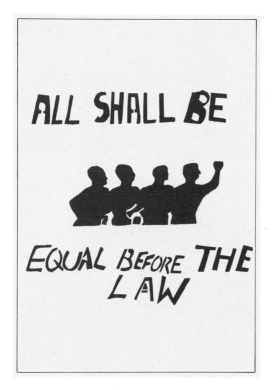

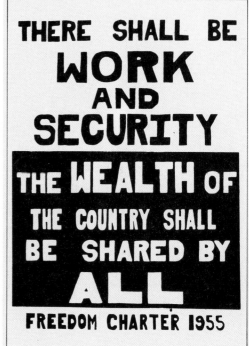

32 1985. The fifth demand of the Freedom Charter.
Silkscreened poster produced by trainees at an STP workshop, Johannesburg
Black

33 1985. The sixth demand of the Freedom Charter.
Silkscreened poster produced by trainees at an STP workshop, Johannesburg
Black

34 1985. The ninth demand of the Freedom Charter.
Silkscreened poster produced by trainees at an STP workshop, Johannesburg
Red

35 1985. The tenth and final demand of the Freedom Charter.
Silkscreened poster produced by trainees at an STP workshop, Johannesburg
Black and red

36 1985. The democratic movement celebrates the 30th anniversary of the Freedom Charter.
Offset litho poster produced by the TIC, Johannesburg
Black and yellow

UDF UNITES - APARTHEID DIVIDES

UDF

UNITED DEMOCRATIC FRONT
FORWARD TO PEOPLES' POWER!

Globe.

Issued by UDF; Khotso House; De Villiers St; JHB.

37 1983. This historic poster was produced for the launch of the UDF in August 1983.
Offset litho poster produced for the UDF by MARS, Johannesburg
Black, red and yellow

38 1984. The first year of the UDF was marked by the unity and action of its 600 affiliates.
Silkscreened poster produced by the UDF at STP, Johannesburg
Black, yellow and red

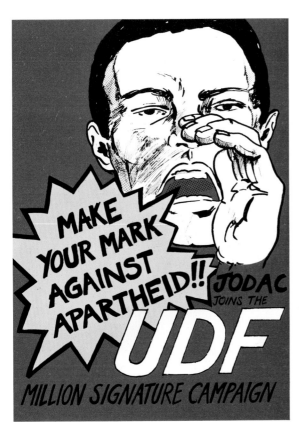

39 1984. Popularising the UDF's first major campaign: to mobilise one million people to sign against apartheid.
Silkscreened poster produced by JODAC at STP, Johannesburg
Black, red and yellow

40 1983. This poster called on people to help build the newly-launched UDF.
Silkscreened poster produced for the UDF at an education and training workshop at CAP
Black

41 1985. First of a set of five posters produced to the highlight the demands
of a consumer boycott in the Western Cape.
Silkscreened poster produced by the UDF at CAP, Cape Town
Black and red

WE DEMAND:
SADF & POLICE OUT OF THE TOWNSHIPS!
U D F SUPPORT THE CONSUMER BOYCOTT!

WE DEMAND:
END THE EMERGENCY! IT'S KILLING US!
U D F SUPPORT THE CONSUMER BOYCOTT!

42 - 45 1985. Four of a set of five posters produced to highlight the demands of a consumer boycott in the Western Cape, including an end to the Emergency and repressive actions by the state.
Silkscreened posters produced by the UDF at CAP, Cape Town
Black and red

WE DEMAND:
FEWER GUNS HIGHER WAGES
U D F SUPPORT THE CONSUMER BOYCOTT!

WE DEMAND:
FREE ALL DETAINEES & POLITICAL PRISONERS!
U D F SUPPORT THE CONSUMER BOYCOTT!

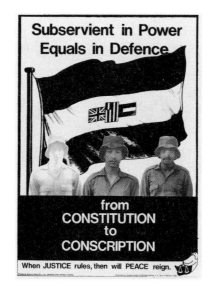

46 c1984. Though coloured and Indian people would have the 'privilege' of being conscripted into the army in return for the vote, they would remain politically subservient to the white government.
Offset litho poster produced by SUCA, Cape Town
Black

47 c1984. Racist elections and military conscription for coloured and Indian people were all that Botha's 'new deal' offered.
Silkscreened poster produced by CAYCO at CAP, Cape Town
Black

48 1984. Coloured South Africans are called on to join the people's extra-parliamentary struggle against racist elections.
Silkscreened poster produced by Transvaal Anti-PC, Johannesburg
Red

49 1984. The UDF organised country-wide rallies (this one in Kimberley, Northern Cape) to mobilise opposition to apartheid elections.
Silkscreened poster produced by the UDF at STP, Johannesburg
Red

Issued by J. de Vries, 3 Hare Street, Mowbray 7700.　　　　　Printed by Esquire Press (Pty) Ltd., Vanguard Drive, Athlone Industria 7764.　Telephone 67-1260/67-1261

50 1984. UDF was formed to oppose the tri-cameral system and all apartheid elections.
Offset litho poster designed for UDF by STP, Johannesburg and printed in Johannesburg and Cape Town
Black, red and yellow

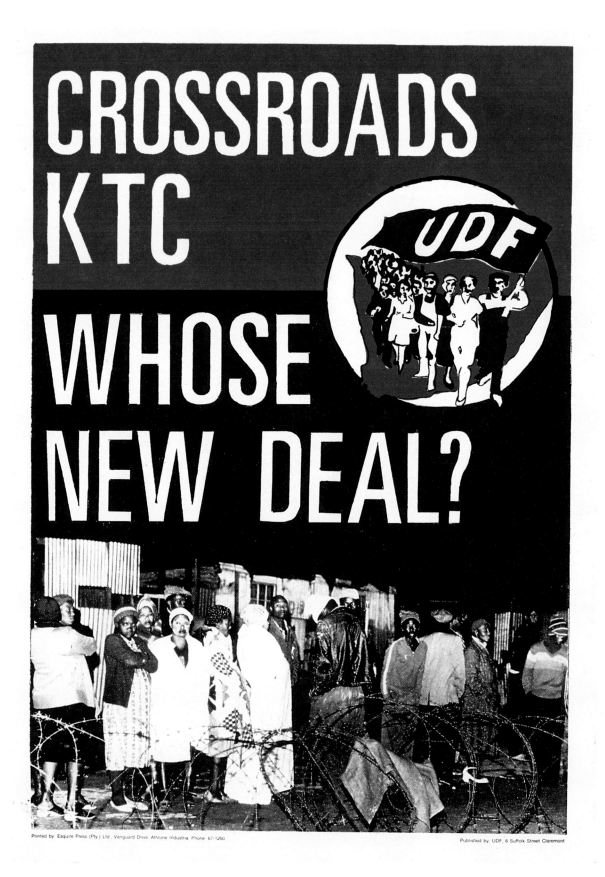

CROSSROADS
KTC
WHOSE
NEW DEAL?

Printed by: Esquire Press (Pty.) Ltd., Vanguard Drive, Athlone Industria Phone 67-1260

Published by: UDF, 6 Suffolk Street Claremont

51 1984. The plight of squatters in the Western Cape continued while the state boasted of 'reforms'.
Offset litho poster issued by UDF, Cape Town
Black and red

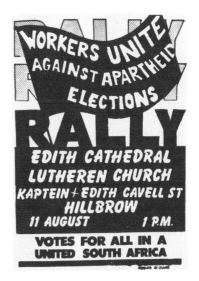

52 1984. The women of South Africa are encouraged to unite against the apartheid government's latest 'deal'.
Silkscreened poster produced by FEDSAW at STP, Johannesburg
Black

53 1984. Community refusal to participate in their own repression.
Silkscreened poster produced by TIC at STP, Johannesburg
Black and green

54 1984. Workers are called upon to unite against apartheid elections.
Silkscreened poster produced by the JUWRC at STP, Johannesburg
Red

55 1983. Township residents are dissuaded from voting for the state's undemocratic community council structures.
Silkscreened poster produced for Soweto Civic Association by the Ad-hoc Poster Group, Johannesburg
Black and yellow

Delmas
Treason Trial

Protest
Meeting

Where : Wits Flower Hall
When : 6 December
Time   : 7:30pm
Speakers: Boesak, Tutu,
              Chikane, Naidoo

We stand by our leaders

56 1988. After a marathon trial, a number of UDF leaders were convicted of treason – the protest
meeting advertised here was banned.
Offset litho poster produced by the Delmas Support Group, Johannesburg
Black, red and yellow

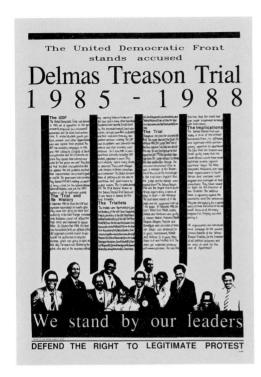

57 1989. This poster was produced as part of the campaign against the conviction of the treason trialists.
Offset litho poster produced by the Delmas Support Group, Johannesburg
Black, red and yellow

The Delmas Treason Trial (text from Poster 57)

The UDF

The United Democratic Front was formed in 1983 out of opposition to the government's proposals for a tricameral parliament and for black local authorities. It united student, youth, political, women's and other organisations who were against these proposals. The UDF ran successful campaigns in 1983 and 1984 calling for a boycott of black local authorities and the tricameral elections. They rejected these schemes and called for 'one person one vote'. They feared that the black local authorities did not address the real problems and that their implementation would lead to greater conflict. The government took no notice. They banned the UDF's meetings, accused it of being a front for the banned African National Congress and put the UDF's leaders in jail for legitimate protest.

The Trial and its History

In September 1984, the fears the UDF had expressed materialised. Six months after they came into office, the black local authority in the Vaal Triangle increased rents. Residents could not afford the high rents and organised to oppose them. On 3 September 1984, the Vaal Civic Association (VCA), an affiliate of the UDF, organised a protest march to persuade the authorities to drop the increase, which was going to start on that day. The march was blocked by the police who shot at the marchers without any warning. Violence broke out in the Vaal and in many other townships. Residents had become frustrated by the increased rentals, bad education, corrupt councillors, no facilities, and their exclusion from any real political decision making. The UDF and its affiliates were blamed for the violence and their members were detained. On 11 June 1985, 22 anti-apartheid activists, including UDF leaders, appeared in court. They had already spent many months in detention. They were charged with treason, murder, terrorism and subversion. The state accused them of plotting with the ANC to overthrow the government by violent means. The trialists denied this. The trial became known as the Delmas Treason Trial, because it was heard in Delmas for the first 18 months.

The Trialists

The trialists were Popo Molefe (37), General Secretary of the UDF, Terror Lekota (39), Publicity Secretary of the UDF, Moss Chikane (40), Transvaal Secretary of the UDF, Tom Manthata (48) from the SACC and the Soweto Civic Association, Gcina Malindi (29), from the Vaal Civic Association (VCA), Patrick Baleka from AZANYU, Oupa Hlomoka (35) from AZAPO, the Reverend Geoff Moselane (42), Petrus Mokoena (50) from the Evaton Ratepayers Association, David Mphuthi (51), Naphtali Nkopane (43), Ephraim Ramakgula (38), Bavumile Vilakazi (32), Johnny Mokoena (36), Simon Nkoli (29), Jake Hlanyane (40), Sam Matlole (64) and Thabiso Ratsomo (31) are all from the Vaal Civic Association and Jerry Thlopane (29) from COSAS.

The Trial

Throughout the trial the accused felt that the judge favoured the state. On 10 March 1987, the Judge 'fired' one of the two assessors who help him decide the case. He was fired because he had signed the UDF's Million Signature Campaign form. The Judge refused to dismiss the other assessor even though the accused complained that he was a member of the Broederbond! How could the trialists get a fair trial when they felt that the Judge and the Assessor were against them? The Delmas treason trial was the longest trial in South African legal history in terms of days in court – over 450 days. The court record consists of 27 194 pages and the Judgement took up 1 521 pages. In November 1988, the court found that Molefe, Lekota, Chikane and Manthata were guilty of treason. Malindi, Mokoena, Mphuthi, Nkopane, Hlanyane, Matlole and Ramakgula were convicted of terrorism. Lekota was sentenced to 12 years imprisonment, Molefe and Chikane to 10 years, Manthata to 6 and Malindi to 5. The others got suspended sentences with severe restrictions. This was the first time that the court had given people suspended sentences with restrictions.

The Implications

The Delmas treason trial was really a trial of the United Democratic Front, its affiliates and legitimate extra-parliamentary opposition to apartheid. The fact that the trialists were found guilty means that the South African courts have made legitimate protest against apartheid illegal. The mass democratic movement, anti-apartheid organisations in South Africa and overseas were angered and outraged at their convictions. They have vowed to fight for the freedom of the trialists. The defence team is appealing against the convictions and the sentences. They are also applying for a special entry to have the whole trial set aside because of the many irregularities they say occurred during it. All organisations and individuals must campaign for the unconditional freedom of the Delmas treason trialists, for the freedom of all political prisoners and we must all work for the end of apartheid.

Note: On appeal the convictions and sentences were set aside and the Delmas trialists are now all free.

58 1989. The Conference for a Democratic Future attempted to unite all organisations involved in the struggle against apartheid.
Offset litho poster produced by the CDF organising committee, Johannesburg
Black, red and yellow

59 1988. The Anti-Apartheid Conference was banned by the state.
Offset litho poster issued by COSATU, Johannesburg
Black and red

60 1989. On 6 September the government held yet another whites-only election while popular organisations were banned and popular leaders imprisoned.
Offset litho poster produced by the MDM, Johannesburg
Black

61 1988. Part of the campaign for a non-racial society, this meeting discussed strategic responses to segregated municipal elections.
Offset litho poster produced by FFF, Johannesburg
Black

62 1988. The '101 Ways to end Apartheid' campaign encouraged people, in particular whites, to take personal responsibility for ending the 'dinosaur' apartheid system.
Offset litho poster produced by FFF, Johannesburg Black on yellow card

63 1985. Concerned Citizens involved a response to the first State of Emergency; their 'Run for Peace' was banned as a 'threat to the security of the state'.
Offset litho poster produced by Concerned Citizens, Johannesburg Black

64 c1987. The FFF programme demands: Freedom from want, Freedom from fear, Freedom of speech and association, Freedom from discrimination and exploitation, and Freedom of conscience.
Offset litho poster produced by FFF, Johannesburg Black

65 1986. Whites are called on to join black South Africans in commemorating the deaths of black students in the June 1976 uprising.
Silkscreened poster produced by JODAC, Johannesburg Black and red

CALL TO WHITES

Public Meeting

"Where to, White Politics?"

: *BEYERS NAUDE*

: *UDF SPEAKER*

: *VAN ZYL SLABBERT*

Jhb City Hall
9 April — 8pm

ISSUED BY JODAC BOX 93118 YEOVILLE

66 1986. The 'Call to Whites' campaign of 1986 emphasised that the South African struggle is not between blacks and whites, but between those who support a non-racial democracy and those who don't.
Offset litho poster produced by JODAC, Johannesburg
Black, red and yellow

An injury to one is an injury to all!

Labour

An injury to one is an injury to all!

Independent trade unions have long been a part of the South African liberation movement. The first black trade union emerged as long ago as 1919, when the Industrial and Commercial Workers Union (ICU) was formed in Cape Town. In succeeding decades it was followed by many others, including the Council of Non-European Trade Unions (CNETU). These unions achieved some gains for their members, but none managed to gain the official recognition the state reserved for white unions.

After the National Party came to power in 1948, black unions found many of their leaders banned from trade union work under the Suppression of Communism Act. Determined to resist, the union movement regrouped and in 1955 formed the South African Congress of Trade Unions (SACTU). In the face of a common onslaught from the government, SACTU joined forces with the African National Congress (ANC) and others to form the Congress Alliance. It reflected their belief that workers' rights could never be adequately defended as long as apartheid existed.

SACTU eventually succumbed to state repression and in the early 1960s, following the Sharpeville massacre and the banning of the ANC, was driven underground. The following ten years were a dark decade for black trade unions.

In the early 1970s, workers began reorganising in Durban. In 1973, mass strikes broke out in support of demands for wage increases. This marked the rebirth of the independent trade union movement.

Unions emerged in the major urban centres of Johannesburg, Durban and Cape Town, and despite intense harassment, managed to survive and grow. The union movement's democratic structures proved resistant to repression, and by 1979 both employers and the state agreed that black unions should be legally recognised. The authorities believed limited recognition would result in more effective control of union activities.

However, the independent unions refused government regulation and continued to organise against low wages and racism, both at work and in the wider society. The Federation of South African Trade Unions (FOSATU), the South African Allied Workers Union (SAAWU), the Western Province General Workers Union (WPGWU), and the Food and Canning Workers Union (FCWU) were among the most prominent of the unions engaged in bitter battles to organise and expand the frontiers of unionisation.

New tactics emerged, including calling on community organisations to support striking workers by boycotting company products. The FCWU used this tactic during the Fattis and Monis strike, as did SAAWU during the Wilson-Rowntree dispute. The early 1980s also saw the 1950s tactic of work stayaways revived.

The emergent unions recognised the need to unite into one trade union federation. But a variety of differences, both organisational and political, made this a lengthy process. During four long years of unity talks, the unions grew rapidly, and new unions, such as the National Union of Mineworkers (NUM), were established.

The political climate within the country also changed. Growing opposition to apartheid resulted in widespread resistance in the face of an intransigent government. This grassroots movement was strengthened by the formation, in 1983, of the United Democratic Front (UDF), which brought together a wide range of anti-apartheid organisations, including a number of the emergent unions. By 1985, most of these emergent trade unions announced themselves ready to unite under the banner of 'One Country, One Federation'.

On 1 December 1985 the Congress of South African Trade Unions (COSATU) was launched in Durban. It brought together 33 unions representing some 450 000 organised workers, making it the largest trade union federation ever formed in South Africa. Elijah Barayi, a mine employee, was elected president, and Jay Naidoo, previously general secretary of the Sweet, Food and Allied Workers Union (SFAWU) was elected general secretary. COSATU openly proclaimed its determination to be politically active: it would fight for a non-racial, democratic South Africa.

Among the policies adopted by COSATU was that of creating one strong union in every industry, by uniting the various smaller unions organising in each sector of the economy. 'One Industry, One Union' became its guiding slogan. In its first five years, COSATU had combined the original 33 affiliates into 13 much larger, stronger, industrial unions.

COSATU's formation also saw a dramatic growth in the number of unionised workers. By mid-1988, COSATU represented some 700 000 workers. Part of this growth stemmed from its policy of organising in sectors where unions were not yet legally recognised. This included organising workers on the farms, in domestic service and, particularly, in the public sector. Membership grew as railway workers, postal workers and others flocked to join the unions. Recognition of these unions was only achieved after lengthy and often bloody battles against a well-armed state. The railway strike of early 1987 brought a measure of recognition to COSATU's railway union, but not before police had killed a number of strikers.

Another COSATU battlefront has been its Living Wage Campaign, with union members involved in major wage strikes in all industries. The most dramatic of these occurred on the mines during mid-1987 when some 350 000 miners downed tools for 21 days. This, the biggest strike in the country's history, hit hard at the core of the economy, the gold mining industry.

The Living Wage Campaign focused not only on wage increases, but also on achieving other changes – public holidays, for example, have been a major battleground. COSATU's members have fought and succeeded in having internationally-celebrated May Day recognised as a public holiday in South Africa. This was achieved only after the federation organised massive work stayaways on 1 May for a number of years. COSATU has also achieved a large measure of success in getting 16 June (the anniversary of the Soweto uprising), and 21 March (the anniversary of the Sharpeville massacre) recognised as public holidays – in fact if not in law.

None of these achievements were easily won. COSATU has existed under an almost continuous State of Emergency which involved intense repression of trade unionists, together with activists in youth, community, religious and political organisations.

A propaganda war aimed at undermining COSATU involved the widespread distribution of dirty tricks pamphlets and posters. And repression did not stop with words: thousands of unionists found themselves detained and held without charge, often for lengthy periods. Others have been assassinated, the victims of secret death squads. Union offices have been raided by police, vandalised, bombed, and burned to the ground. The most vicious attack occurred in May 1987 when COSATU's headquarters in Johannesburg were destroyed in a massive explosion. The police have still failed to apprehend the perpetrators of any of these attacks.

Repression failed to intimidate either COSATU or its affiliated unions. As a result, more systematic attacks were launched against it in 1988. In February, the government restricted COSATU from any participation in politics, at the same time banning the UDF. Breach of these regulations was punishable by heavy jail sentences and fines. In addition the government, at the urging of employers, introduced a new labour law. The Labour Relations Amendment Act aimed at reversing many reforms introduced in 1979. Both the restrictions and the new labour law fostered greater unity among COSATU affiliates. There was widespread defiance of the restrictions on its political activities – the new labour law, although promulgated, was rendered largely a dead letter. Two major national stayaways were central to achieving this. One stayaway lasted three days, and in both, millions rallied to COSATU's defence. These stayaways were conducted jointly with many non-COSATU unions, in particular those affiliated to the National Council of Trade Unions (NACTU).

Not all COSATU's activities have been so spectacular. Like trade unions worldwide, it has involved itself in the normal range of bread-and-butter activities. It has attempted, with a large measure of success, to draw unions outside COSATU into its ranks. It has tried to harness militant rural workers into disciplined unions. It has developed links internationally, and played an important part in assisting the development of independent unions in Namibia.

COSATU unions have taken up health and safety issues. The miners' union, NUM, is particularly active in this regard. The dangers facing mineworkers were demonstrated by an horrific accident during September 1986, when 177 workers died at Kinross gold mine.

Since its inception, COSATU has been politically active. In 1987 it adopted the Freedom Charter, thereby aligning itself with the non-racial, democratic perspective of the ANC. With the unbanning of political organisations in February 1990, these links strengthened.

COSATU has stressed both its determination to remain politically active in the search for democracy, as well as its desire to remain independent. This has involved retaining its strongly separate identity, but entering into a strategic alliance with both the ANC and SACP.

Today COSATU is widely recognised, by friend and foe alike, as one of the pillars of the liberation movement. It now represents over a million workers, with organisation expanding daily. Its existence is a challenge to a post-apartheid South Africa. The majority of South Africans want not only political rights – they also demand social and economic justice. ❏

EVERY WORKER A UNION MEMBER

5 March 1955 — 1990 35th Anniversary of the South African Congress of Trade Unions

MATHIBE PRINTERS 933-1323

67 1990. SACTU celebrated its 35th anniversary by issuing this and three other posters – the first the organisation had produced openly inside the country since the 1960s.
Offset litho poster produced by SACTU, Johannesburg
Full colour

68 1984. FOSATU advertises a meeting of its Johannesburg local.
Silkscreened poster produced by FOSATU at STP, Johannesburg
Black, red and yellow

69 1984. MAWU announces its Transvaal AGM.
Silkscreened poster produced by MAWU at STP, Johannesburg
Black

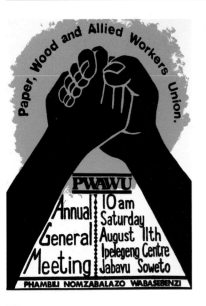

70 1984. Poster for PWAWU's AGM.
Silkscreened poster produced by PWAWU at STP, Johannesburg
Red and green

71 1984. CLOWU uses a cartoon to educate workers.
Silkscreened poster produced for CLOWU by CAP, Cape Town
Black and green

73 1984. SAAWU advertises its Annual General Meeting. *Silkscreened poster produced by SAAWU at STP, Johannesburg Black and green*

72 1984. RAWU poster for the union's AGM. *Silkscreened poster produced by CAP for RAWU, Cape Town Black and red*

74 1985. Progressive unions celebrate SACTU's 30th anniversary. *Offset litho produced by the Inter-union Co-ordinating Committee through STP, Johannesburg Black*

SOUTH AFRICAN SCOOTER DRIVERS UNION

75 1984. SASDU takes off!
Silkscreened poster produced by SASDU at STP, Johannesburg
Black, yellow and red

BOYCOTT THE CAN!

SOFT DRINK and BEER CANS

- The Management of Metal Box retrenched 22 black workers and after a week hired 3 white workers.
- On the 22 October 1985 workers went on strike demanding the dismissal of the three workers, and that workers should be hired from the retrenched ones.
- On the 11th November 1985 Metal Box dismissed the whole workforce of 500 people.
- Workers of Metal Box are calling upon fellow working people in townships and rural areas to boycott products of Metal Box.

WE CALL UPON ALL WORKERS, WORKER ORGANISATIONS, STUDENTS AND PROGRESSIVE ORGANISATIONS TO BOYCOTT METAL BOX PRODUCTS IN SOLIDARITY WITH THE DISMISSED WORKERS.

WE DEMAND OUR JOBS BACK!

METAL BOX WORKERS

AN INJURY TO ONE IS AN INJURY TO ALL

76 1985. Metal Box workers call on unions and the community to boycott Metal Box products in support of striking workers.

Offset litho poster issued by Metal Box Support Committee through STP, Johannesburg

Black, red and yellow

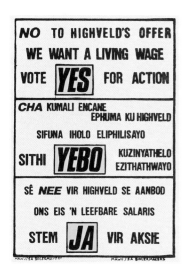

77 1984. An appeal to Highveld Steel workers to reject the company's wage offer and vote 'yes' for union action in support of a living wage.
Silkscreened poster produced by MAWU and the SA Boilermakers' Society at STP, Johannesburg
Black and yellow

78 1981. Johannesburg concert held in support of striking Wilson-Rowntree workers in East London – as part of the 'Boycott Wilson-Rowntree sweets' campaign.
Silkscreened poster produced by the Wilson-Rowntree Support Committee, Johannesburg
Black

79 1986. Demanding the unconditional reinstatement of striking workers at the Da Gama textile factory in the Cape.
Silkscreened poster produced by Saldanha Youth Congress at CAP, Cape Town
Black and red

80 1984. Simba workers roar their discontent with management during a strike.
Silkscreened poster produced for SFAWU by Simba Workers Committee at STP, Johannesburg
Red

81 1985. Poster celebrating the launch of COSATU and its call for 'One country, one federation'.

Offset litho poster produced for COSATU in Cape Town

Full colour

82 1985. COSATU launch poster.
Offset litho poster produced by the Unity Unions, Durban
Black and red

83 1988. The Special Congress of COSATU discussed proposed amendments to the Labour Relations Act and restrictions placed on the federation under Emergency regulations.
Offset litho poster produced by COSATU, Johannesburg
Black, red and yellow

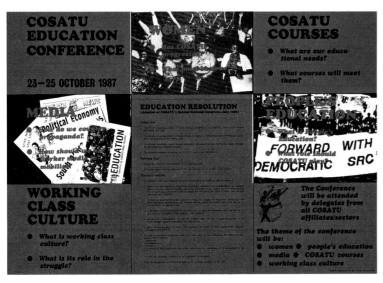

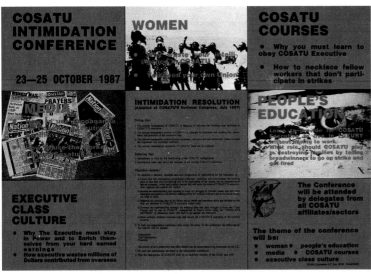

84 – 85 1987. COSATU's first Education Conference. Poster 84 was produced to advertise the event. Poster 85 was produced by unknown parties to undermine COSATU and sabotage the conference.
Offset litho posters, No 84 produced by COSATU Black and red

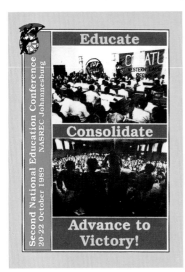

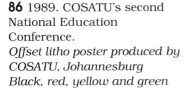

86 1989. COSATU's second National Education Conference.
Offset litho poster produced by COSATU, Johannesburg Black, red, yellow and green

87 1987. Second National Congress of COSATU.
Offset litho produced by COSATU, Johannesburg Full colour

88 1989. Third National Congress of COSATU.
Offset litho produced by COSATU in Johannesburg Black, red and yellow

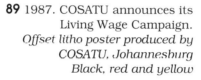

89 1987. COSATU announces its
Living Wage Campaign.
*Offset litho poster produced by
COSATU, Johannesburg
Black, red and yellow*

90 1989. SADWU advertises Living
Wage rallies in different parts
of the country.
*Offset litho poster produced for SADWU
by TOPS/COSATU
Black and orange*

91 1989. COSATU mass rally in
support of the Anti-Labour Relations
Act Campaign.
*Offset litho poster produced by COSATU
at CAP, Cape Town
Black and red*

92 1989. Anti-Labour Relations Act
Campaign poster issued
by COSATU and NACTU.
*Offset litho poster produced by
COSATU, Johannesburg
Black and yellow*

93 1987. NUM gives support to the Living Wage Campaign
during the national mineworkers' strike.
Offset litho poster produced for NUM, Johannesburg
Black, red and yellow

94 1987. NUM celebrates the end of the national miners' strike.
Offset litho poster produced for NUM, Johannesburg
Black and yellow

WORKERS UNITE FOR INDEPENDENCE!

MAY DAY NAMIBIA ·1989·

Build solidarity action with Namibian workers and youth

95 1989. May Day poster saluting Namibian independence – produced simultaneously by NUNW in Namibia and COSATU in Johannesburg.
Offset litho poster reproduced by COSATU, Johannesburg
Black, red, green and blue

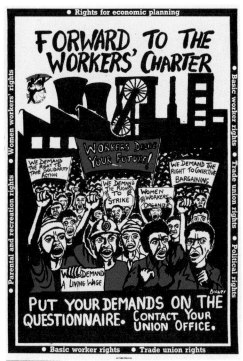

96 c1988. NUMSA demands the release of its general secretary and four other activists.
Offset litho poster produced for NUMSA, Johannesburg
Black, blue and red

97 1990. COSATU urges workers to help draft a Workers' Charter.
Offset litho poster produced by COSATU, Johannesburg
Black and red

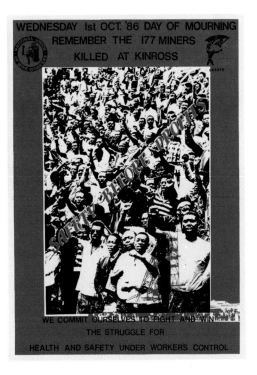

98 1987. The 'Hands-off COSATU' campaign followed the bombing of the federation's headquarters and the killing of striking railway workers.
Offset litho poster produced by COSATU, Johannesburg
Black and red

99 1986. NUM poster condemns the death of 177 mineworkers due to unsafe working conditions.
Offset litho poster produced by NUM, Johannesburg
Black and red

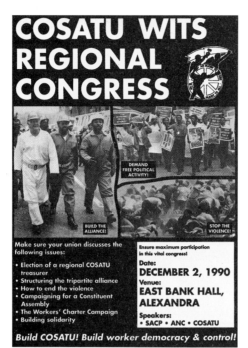

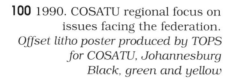

100 1990. COSATU regional focus on issues facing the federation.
Offset litho poster produced by TOPS for COSATU, Johannesburg
Black, green and yellow

101 1989. COSATU participates in International Literacy Day.
Offset litho poster produced by COSATU/TOPS, Johannesburg
Black and green

102 1989. Domestic and agricultural workers have never been protected by labour legislation.
Offset litho poster produced by COSATU, Johannesburg
Black and red

103 1988. COSATU recognises the need to pay special attention to the organising of women workers.
Offset litho poster produced by Gardens Media Group/CAP for COSATU, Johannesburg
Black, red and yellow

104 1988. The Wits Region of NUMSA holds a general meeting for women workers.
Offset litho poster produced by NUMSA, Johannesburg
Blue and black

105 1988. Poster advertising a regional women's congress organised by COSATU's Northern Transvaal structure.
Offset litho poster produced by COSATU, Johannesburg
Black and red

106 1988. PPWAWU announces its National Congress.
Offset litho poster produced by COSATU for PPWAWU, Johannesburg
Black, green and red

107 1987. CCAWUSA calls for support for strikers at OK Bazaars, one of South Africa's largest retail chains.
Silkscreened poster produced by CCAWUSA at CAP, Cape Town
Black and red

Consolidate our gains & advance to a living wage

PPWAWU CONGRESS

8 - 11 September 1988
Pietermaritzburg

● Presidential speech ● Annual report ●
● Financial Report ● Resolutions ● Elections ●

HIGH PROFIT LOW WAGES: NOT OK!

SUPPORT THE STRUGGLE FOR A LIVING WAGE!

VIVA CCAWUSA VIVA COSATU

•SIGN THE STOP ORDER FORM NOW!!

HAVE YOU JOINED NUM?

NUM FIGHTS FOR: •A living wage •Decent housing and an end to the compound system •Better health and safety •No job reservation or racism •More control at the workplace •Unity
Every mineworker a NUM member

Support the strikers!

SOLIDARITY!

108 1989. SAMWU strike poster with political demands opposing town councils imposed on communities by the state.
Offset litho poster produced by TOPS for SAMWU, Johannesburg
Black and red

109 1989. NUM encourages workers to join the union.
Offset litho poster produced by NUM, Johannesburg
Yellow and black

METAL
WAGE TALKS 1988

SEIFSA offers 11 -14% - a R2,95 minimum

DEADLOCKED

WORKERS POWER

IMF demands R1 across the board - a R4 minimum

IMF general meetings will be held on 11th and 25th June

GLOBE

110 1988. International Metalworkers Federation meetings held in the wake of a wage deadlock between NUMSA and employers.
Offset litho poster produced by NUMSA, Johannesburg
Black, red and green

RACIST HOTEL BOSSES!

REINSTATE THE WORKERS YOU FIRED FOR OBSERVING JUNE 16 VIVA CCAWUSA! VIVA COSATU!

Issued by: CCAWUSA, WANDERERS STREET, JOHANNESBURG

Globe

111 1989. Hotel workers were dismissed after staying away on 16 June – South African workers demand recognition of 16 June as an official public holiday.
Offset litho poster produced by CCAWUSA, Johannesburg
Black, red and yellow

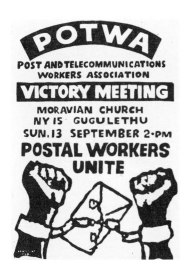

112 1988. POTWA, then an in-house union, but today a COSATU affiliate, celebrates a strike victory.
Silkscreened poster produced at CAP, Cape Town
Black

113 c1989. FAWU exposes the oppressive working conditions on a tea estate and demands union recognition.
Offset litho poster produced by FAWU, Durban
Green and black

114 1987. TGWU general poster.
Offset litho poster produced by TGWU, Johannesburg
Black, blue and red

115 1989. Pro-strike, anti-scab poster by FAWU and COSATU during the strike at Spekenham, a meat processing plant.
Silkscreened poster produced by FAWU, Cape Town
Black

116 1991. Although issued in 1991 as the first SACP May Day poster produced legally inside the country since 1950, this was painted in prison by an ANC member during 1990.
Offset litho poster issued by the SACP, Johannesburg
Full colour

117 1988. May Day poster in Zulu advertises a meeting in Durban.
Offset litho poster
issued by UDF, Durban
Black and red

118 1986. UDF calls for May Day to be declared a public holiday.
Offset litho poster produced by the UDF, Johannesburg
Red, black and yellow

119 1984. JODAC supports recognition of May Day as a public holiday.
Silkscreened poster produced by JODAC at STP, Johannesburg
Black and red printed on brown wrapping paper

120 1989. COSATU celebrates May Day and popularises the federation's Living Wage Campaign.
Offset litho poster designed by Gardens Media Group/CAP, Cape Town and produced by COSATU,
Johannesburg
Black, red and yellow

121 1989. May Day is ours! The first of a set of five posters celebrating May Day.
Silkscreened poster produced by Gardens Media Group at CAP, Cape Town
Black

IN THE MINES

MAYDAY IS OURS!

122 - 125 1989. After decades of struggle by the working class, 1 May – May Day – has finally been recognised as an official public holiday in South Africa.
Silkscreened posters produced by Gardens Media Project at CAP, Cape Town
Black

ON THE LAND

MAYDAY IS OURS!

IN THE FACTORIES

MAYDAY IS OURS!

IN THE STREETS

MAYDAY IS OURS!

126 c1988. Health and safety poster.
Offset litho poster produced by members of the Industrial Health Research Group
Full colour

127 c1985. The struggle for healthy and safe working conditions continues.
Offset litho poster produced by the Industrial Health Unit of the Department of Sociology at the University of Natal in Durban
Black and red

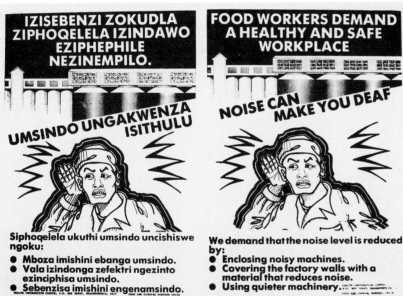

IZISEBENZI ZOKUDLA ZIPHOQELELA IZINDAWO EZIPHEPHILE NEZINEMPILO.

FOOD WORKERS DEMAND A HEALTHY AND SAFE WORKPLACE

UMSINDO UNGAKWENZA ISITHULU

NOISE CAN MAKE YOU DEAF

Siphoqelela ukuthi umsindo uncishiswe ngoku:
● **Mboza imishini ebanga umsindo.**
● **Vala izindonga zefektri ngezinto ezinciphisa umsindo.**
● **Sebenzisa imishini engenamsindo.**

We demand that the noise level is reduced by:
● **Enclosing noisy machines.**
● **Covering the factory walls with a material that reduces noise.**
● **Using quieter machinery.**

128 1985. The dangers of noise in the workplace.
Silkscreened poster produced at STP by HIC for FCWU, Johannesburg
Black

MATERNITY RIGHTS FOR WORKING WOMEN

We demand the right to:
● work when we are pregnant
● work in safe conditions
● time off to attend ante-natal clinics
● look after our babies for at least 6 months
● get paid while we are away
● come back to our jobs without loss of benefits
● paternity leave for working men
(when their babies are born)

HEALTH INFORMATION CENTRE.
1 Melle House, 31 Melle St.,
Braamfontein.
PO Box 30869, Braamfontein, 2017
Tel No 339 7411

129 1985. Women workers list their minimum demands for maternity rights.
Offset litho poster produced by HIC, Johannesburg
Red and black

Azikhwelwa: we will not ride!

Community

Azikhwelwa - we will not ride!

The 1980s will be remembered as the decade during which the pillars of apartheid began to crumble in the face of popular insurrection. Apartheid is not simply a constitutional order that structures political life – it is also a social order that regulates the daily lives of South African people. This regulation is particularly repressive for black people: where they live, how they live, where they work, where their children are educated – all are determined by apartheid laws.

During the 1980s grassroots social movements arose, mobilising and organising communities around three primary issues:

❑ services, housing and land;
❑ grassroots political democracy; and
❑ building new communities, ie an embryonic alternative social order.

Beginning with the formation of the Port Elizabeth Black Civic Organisation (PEBCO) and the Soweto Civic Association (SCA) in 1979, 'civics' sprang up in communities across the country. The 1980 schools boycott in the Western Cape provided the impetus for Cape Town's neighbourhood-based civic movement. In Natal, from 1982 onwards, bus boycotts and rent struggles gave rise to civics in both the African and Indian areas.

When the UDF was founded in 1983, civics came together under this national umbrella body, and began to spread even more rapidly, with the Border and Eastern Cape regions becoming the best organised.

The 1985-86 consumer boycotts welded these separate civic organisations into an effective regional movement.

The Cradock Residents' Organisation led the way by emulating the 1950s 'M Plan'-organisation based on street committees, initiated by Nelson Mandela after the Defiance Campaign in 1952. This mode of organisation became a model for the rest of the country in the late 1980s.

Organisation took off quickly in the small Border and Eastern Cape towns during the 1983-85 period, but it took much longer to filter through the huge urban sprawls and far-flung rural communities in the Transvaal.

The Transvaal regional stayaway in November 1984 paved the way for subsequent united union and community action. But despite the existence of civics in the Northern, Eastern and Southern Transvaal, it was not until the 1986 Transvaal rent boycotts that a Transvaal civic movement emerged with a sense of identity and explicit goals.

In the Bloemfontein area, South Africa's second largest township, Botshabelo, became the focus of a civic movement that linked local issues to resistance against incorporation into the QwaQwa bantustan.

Even smaller rural townships such as Huhudi, near Vryburg, saw community structures develop. Often mobilisation occurred when residents were confronted by a specific problem. In Huhudi, people were threatened with removal from their homes to a location far away within the borders of the Bophuthatswana bantustan.

By grassroots social movements we refer to the classic combination of local organisations: a civic or residents' organisation concerned with general community matters; a youth congress for the unemployed youth and young workers; a students' congress for school pupils; a women's organisation; an education committee of some kind (a parent-teacher-student association or crisis committee); a trade union local in the larger areas; and a string of local ad hoc issue-oriented committees, ranging from a commuter committee if there is a bus boycott, a consumer boycott committee, a squatters' committee, or an anti-removals committee. In many areas local progressive professional associations – lawyers, doctors, teachers, welfare officers, mental health workers and academics – worked together with the civic structures.

There were no rules as to which organisation should be dominant. Agreed direction was formulated by the leadership of different organisations working together. These were usually a combination of workers, youth, students, organised women and professionals. In certain areas, township-wide co-ordinating structures were established to bring all the organisations together.

The most significant feature of these social movements is that they established deeply rooted structures that brought ordinary people into the decision-making process for the first time. This was done via the street and area committee system. Each street would, at a broad-based house meeting, elect a street committee, which in turn sent representatives to an area (or zone) committee.

The area committees were represented on a township-wide co-ordinating committee. These co-ordinating committees usually began defensively, to protect the community from state repression and sometimes crime. However, in many areas these structures laid the basis for innovative, pro-active development strategies. This network of social movements began to break down apartheid-imposed structures and recreate communities according to democratic principles.

Many community struggles developed in protest against apartheid regulation of basic urban necessities: housing, land, services (such as water and sewerage), transport, health care, child care, and education. This struggle clashed head-on with local government structures, which are notoriously corrupt, elected on extremely low polls (where elections took place at all), administratively inefficient and fiscally unviable.

Protest would begin on a small scale via petitions, representations and press statements. When authorities ignored these representations, wider collective resources were mobilised in marches, stayaways, boycott action and so forth. Inevitably, such actions were met by harsh security force action, in turn triggering the familiar cycle of protest-repression-violence-counter-violence. The States of Emergency, first declared in 1985 and lasting effectively until mid-1989, were clearly aimed at destroying these grassroots social movements. Meetings and organisations were banned, activists detained and jailed, and army troops patrolled township streets.

As the cycle escalated, grassroots organisation gained a firmer hold, leading eventually – in a few townships – to a situation which was popularly perceived as one of 'dual power' between civic structures and state-run local government. Communities could only take control of their areas for short periods, while under continual attack by the state. However, there were many cases where situations of 'dual power' led to negotiations with local-level white business interests and local authorities achieving some redress for black communities.

As well as challenging the state, grassroots social movements also helped to redefine social and cultural relationships within the community. New roles for women in public life emerged; the relationships between generations was continually contested, debated and reformulated; conceptions of citizenship emerged premised on participation rather than helpless passivity; streets and suburbs were renamed after popular symbols and leaders; solidarity against crime became a norm and outsiders seeking to co-opt allies and divide the community were vehemently opposed. In short, communities moved towards forging identities that opposed the logic, values and interests apartheid sought to impose on them.

Indeed, out of this frequently violent confrontation between local governments and the communities emerged a commitment to local democracy that will help shape a future constitutional order.

Since the national detainees' hunger strike in February 1989, popular civic-type organisations have begun to recover from the near-mortal blows many suffered during the Emergency. Throughout the country, the various complex regional movements with their own histories, styles, personalities and issues have begun to re-emerge. This is testimony to the durability of civil society, which, if it continues to develop as it has to date, should provide a sound and robust foundation for a future democratic and just South Africa. ❏

KRUGERSDORP RESIDENTS' ORGANISATION

RESIDENTS MEETING

Dr MOTLANA THE ROLE OF CIVIC ASSOCIATIONS

ISAAC GENU PROBLEMS IN KAGISO & MUNSIEVILLE

27/1/85

12 NOON

ROMAN CATHOLIC CHURCH

KAGISO 2

ISSUED BY KRO AD-HOC COMM

130 1985. Krugersdorp residents discuss civic issues.
Silkscreened poster produced by KRO Ad-Hoc Committee at STP, Johannesburg
Black and yellow

131 c1985. Announcement of a meeting to discuss community problems in Rockville.
Silkscreened poster produced by Rockville Civic Association at STP, Johannesburg
Red

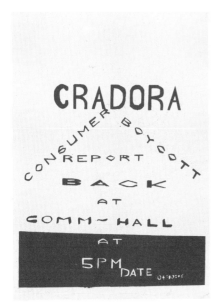

132 c 1985. Cradock residents are called to a report-back meeting on a consumer boycott in the town.
Silkscreened poster produced by CRADORA during a training workshop at STP, Johannesburg
Red

133 1984. A meeting called to protest PW Botha's 'new deal'.
Silkscreened poster produced at CAP by the Anti-Election Group of Ravensmead, Cape Town
Black and yellow

134 1984. Meeting on price rises and political elections – the poster is in Afrikaans, the most common language used by coloured people in the Cape.
Silkscreened poster produced for Elsie's River Civic at CAP, Cape Town
Black and red

135 1985. Mass rally to discuss the State of Emergency, and consumer and school boycotts.
Silkscreened poster produced by the Athlone Action Committee at CAP, Cape Town
Black

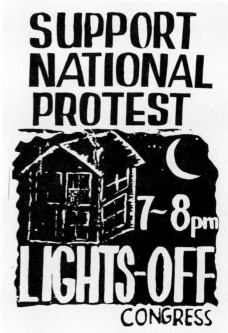

136 1984. This stayaway was in response to repression following the uprising of 3 September.
Silkscreened poster produced by Tvl Stayaway Committee at STP, Johannesburg
Red

137 c1986. A call for community support of a lights-out campaign against repression.
Silkscreened poster produced by the TIC at STP, Johannesburg
Black

138 1987. CAYCO identifies with COSATU and striking workers from FAWU.
Offset litho poster produced by CAYCO
Black and red

139 1986. 'We are not going to Khayelitsha' – the slogan of residents of Cape Town's black areas forced to leave their homes by the state.
Silkscreened poster produced for UWO at CAP, Cape Town
Black and green

STOP LAWAAIKAMP REMOVALS

140 1987. Cartoon comment on the pending forced removal of coloured residents from Lawaaikamp.
Offset litho poster produced by SPP/DAG at CAP, Cape Town
Black and red

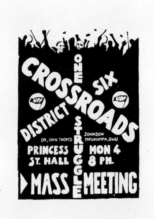

141 c1986. The UDF draws attention to the link between struggles against removals by the people of Crossroads and District Six.
Silkscreened poster produced by the UDF at CAP, Cape Town
Black

143 1986. 'We are not going to Kwa Nobuhle' – the people of Langa in the Eastern Cape demand housing for all.
Silkscreened poster produced for Langa residents at STP, Johannesburg
Black

142 c1986. A squatters' prayer: 'The Lord of mercy is my best guide. He shall raise the humble and humble the powerful'.
Offset litho poster produced by Ecumenical Action Movement
Black and green

144 1985. Calendar depicting the struggle of Huhudi community against removals and poor living conditions.
Silkscreened poster produced by members of the HCA at STP, Johannesburg
Black, blue, red and green (marbled)

HUHUDI YOUTH ORGANISATION

PUDUMONG

NO TO HUNGER
NO TO HIGH RENTS
NO TO PUDUMONG!

145 1985. Huhudi youth back community resistance to forced removal – after
many years of struggle, the people of Huhudi won permission to stay.
*Silkscreened poster produced by the HUYO at Huhudi's own workshop which was
subsequently petrol-bombed by unknown attackers*
Red

146 1985. Huhudi community holds a
rally in support of their detained
leaders.
*Silkscreened poster produced by the
people of Huhudi at their own workshop*
Black, red and yellow

147 1984. Huhudi organisations host a
day of cultural events.
*Silkscreened poster produced by the
HUYO at STP, Johannesburg*
Black, red and yellow (marbled)

148 1988. Meeting to discuss the campaign against the Group Areas Act and segregated areas.
Offset litho poster produced for ACTSTOP, Johannesburg
Black, green and yellow

149 c1988. Call for the opening of a hospital which stood empty after construction was completed, even though its facilities were urgently needed.
Silkscreened poster produced by the people of Lenasia
Black

150 1989. Notice of a seminar on housing and the homeless question in the Western Cape.
Silkscreened poster produced by the Help the Homeless Committee at CAP, Cape Town
Blue and brown

151 1989. A youth congress based in a white area opposes the Group Areas Act and popularises the Freedom Charter's call for houses for all.
Silkscreened poster produced by GAYCO at CAP, Cape Town
Black, red and yellow

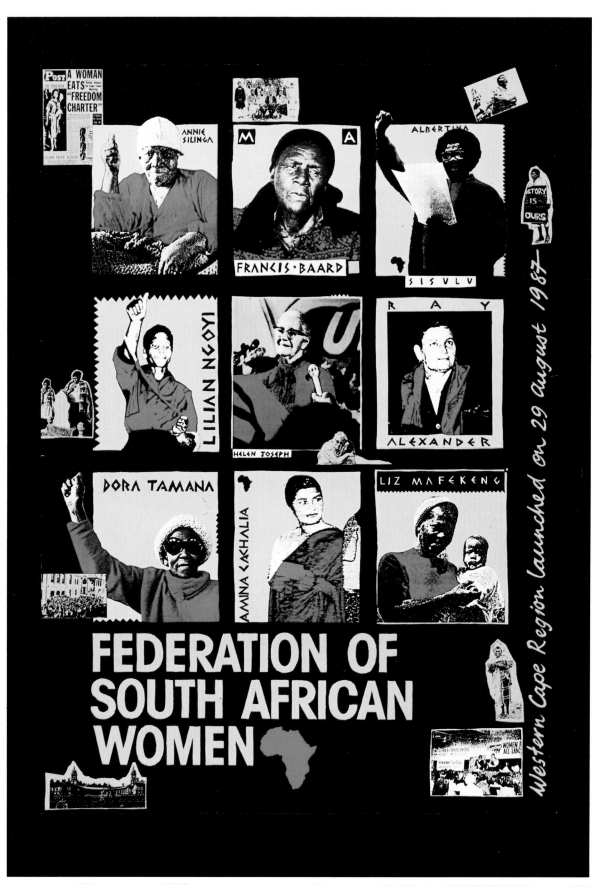

152 1987. Leading women in the South African struggle are honoured at the launch of the Western Cape Region of FEDSAW.

Offset litho poster produced by FEDSAW, Western Cape
Black, green and yellow

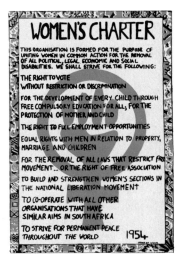

153 c1984. Celebrating the role of women in the struggle and challenging male exploitation of women.
Offset litho poster produced by Learn and Teach, Johannesburg
Black

154 c1987. The Women's Charter of 1954 sets out proposed rights for women in a free and non-sexist society.
Silkscreened poster by the Women's Movement, Wits University, Johannesburg
Black and green

155 1984. Celebrating 9 August 1956 when 20 000 women delivered a petition against racism to the government in Pretoria.
Silkscreened poster produced at CAP, Cape Town
Black and red

156 c1988. This slogan poster became the rallying cry of women's organisations – the picture is of women marching to government offices at the Union Buildings, Pretoria in 1956.
Silkscreened poster produced at CAP, Cape Town
Black, green and red

157 1987. 'Go well' – farewell to a woman comrade who died in the service of the struggle.
Offset litho poster produced for UWCO at CAP, Cape Town
Black

158 1984. Activist Dorothy Nyembe was released from prison after a 15-year sentence.
Silkscreened poster produced at STP for FEDSAW, Johannesburg
Black and green

159 1985. Albertina Sisulu, UDF president, was subpoenaed to give evidence against her nephew, on trial for liberation movement activities.
Offset litho poster issued by FEDTRAW, Johannesburg
Black and red

160 c1988. Many women have been detained as a result of their contribution to the struggle (this poster was commissioned by DPSC, but had to be issued by FEDRAW after DPSC was restricted).
Offset litho poster produced by TOPS for DPSC, Johannesburg
Black and red

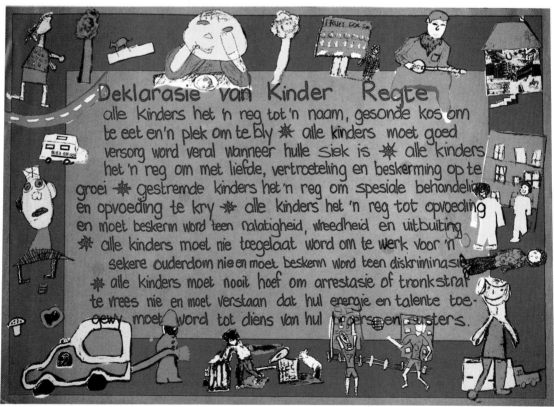

161 1987. **162** 1987. English and Afrikaans versions of the International Declaration of Children's Rights printed at a time when hundreds of children were in detention.

Offset litho poster produced by the Free the Children Alliance, Johannesburg
Black, red, yellow, blue and green
Offset litho poster produced by Molo Songololo, a children's magazine in Cape Town
Pink, blue, green and yellow

163 1987. May Day is as important for children as it is for their parents.
Silkscreened poster produced by Children's Resource Centre at CAP, Cape Town
Black, red, yellow, blue and green

164 c1986. A jazz evening to raise awareness and financial support.
Offset litho poster produced by the Free the Children Alliance, Johannesburg
Black and red

165 1986. The community celebrates 1 June, International Children's Day.
Silkscreened poster produced by Molo Songololo at CAP, Cape Town
Black, blue and red

166 c1987. An Easter church service held to protest against children being held in detention.
Offset litho poster produced in Cape Town
Black

167 c1989. The youth identify with the demands of the Freedom Charter.

Offset litho poster
Black, red, green and yellow

168 1986. A youth congress reaffirms its opposition to apartheid's tri-cameral parliament.
Silkscreened poster produced by SAYCO during a CAP training workshop in Saldanha
Red

169 1987. SAYCO highlights political prisoners on death row. Some of those on death row were convicted on the basis of 'common purpose', whereby an accused can be found guilty if it is proved that he or she was part of the crowd which committed the crime.
Offset litho poster produced by SAYCO Western Cape region
Black and yellow

170 1987. A Spring Fair in Cape Town.
Offset litho poster produced by the Mowbray Youth Congress
Black and pink

171 1987. A Cape Town youth congress celebrates 16 December – Heroes' Day – when Umkhonto was launched in 1961.
Offset litho poster produced by GAYCO, Cape Town
Black and yellow

REGIONAL YOUTH CONGRESS

WE SAY:

NO TO FORCED REMOVALS

NO TO HIGH RENTS

FORWARD TO THE PEOPLE'S GOVERNMENT

172 1984. The youth lay out their demands.
Silkscreened poster produced at STP by trainee youth screen-printers
Black

173 1985. The churches mobilise the youth during International Youth Year.
Offset litho poster produced by the Churches IYY Committee, Johannesburg
Black, yellow and orange

174 1987. A soccer match held in memory of an activist.
Silkscreened poster produced by CAYCO, Bonteheuwel, at CAP, Cape Town
Red

175 1984. UDF calls on the youth to reject apartheid elections.
Silkscreened poster produced by UDF student and youth affiliates at STP, Johannesburg
Red

176 1985. The United Nations-sponsored International Youth Year helped progressive youth structures to recruit and organise new members.
Silkscreened poster produced by the IYY Co-ordinating Committee, Johannesburg at STP
Black, red and blue

177 c1987. Churches express solidarity with the workers' struggle.
Offset litho poster produced by the Labour Programme of Diakonia, Durban
Black, red and yellow

People in Pain

How long will you and I be silent?

Printed by Esquire Press (Pty.) Ltd. Vanguard Drive, Athlone Industria   Published by Student Union for Christian Action

178 1985. A challenge to speak out against suffering caused by repression.
Offset litho poster produced by SUCA, Cape Town
Black

Workers have a right to receive a
LIVING WAGE

Labourers have mowed your fields and you have cheated them. Listen to the wages that you kept back calling out. Realise that the cries of those who gather in your crops have reached the ears of the Lord of Hosts.   James 5:4

179 c1984. The right of workers to a living wage is supported by a quotation from the bible.
Offset litho poster produced by Diakonia Church and Industry Programme, Durban
Black

Upholding Christian and Civilized Standards...

180 1985. The cruelty of a so-called Christian state.
Offset litho poster produced by SUCA, Cape Town
Black

TRULY, I SAY TO YOU, AS YOU DID IT NOT TO ONE OF THE LEAST OF THESE, YOU DID IT NOT TO ME
MATTHEW 25 : 45

181 1985. A challenge to Christians for their actions against fellow humans.
Offset litho poster produced for WPCC at CAP, Cape Town
Black

182 1986. Different religious groups unite to protest against the detention of children under the State of Emergency.
Offset litho poster produced by Black Sash, Johannesburg
Black and red

183 c1986. South African Muslims identify with political detainees.
Silkscreened poster produced by the Call of Islam at CAP, Cape Town
Black and red

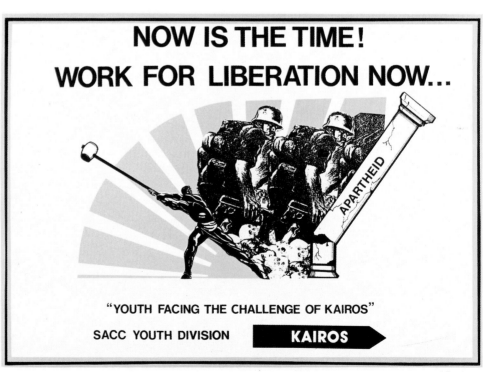

184 1985. A call for Christian youth to join the struggle against apartheid.
Offset litho poster produced by the SACC Youth Division, Johannesburg
Black and yellow

JEWS FOR SOCIAL JUSTICE

invite you to a

PESACH PUBLIC MEETING

Titled

FROM SLAVERY TO FREEDOM

- THEN AND NOW

SPEAKERS : Rabbi Ady E. Assabi
Rabbi Lewis Furman
Rose Zwi - Prizewinning authoress
Raymond Suttner - Senior law lecturer
WITS.
Ex-political detainee

Sunday 20th April · 7·30 pm
H.O.D. Hall · 55 Gardens Road · Orchards

Issued by Jews for Social Justice

185 1986. Progressive Jewish group holds meeting to focus on the universal struggle for freedom.
Silkscreened poster produced for Jews for Social Justice by STP, Johannesburg
Blue

NOBEL PEACE PRIZE WINNER

1984

UDF CELEBRATES

MUSIC . DANCING . SPEAKERS

Free ~ All welcome

JABULANI AMPHITHEATRE

10 FEBRUARY 1985

10am

UDF

186 1985. Democratic organisations honour Bishop Desmond Tutu, winner of the Nobel Peace Prize.
Offset litho poster produced for the UDF by STP, Johannesburg
Black and red

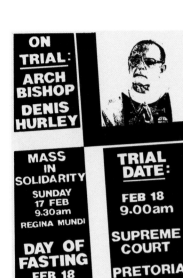

187 1985. The Catholic Church backs Archbishop Denis Hurley, on trial as a result of his anti-apartheid stance.
Silkscreened poster produced at STP, Johannesburg
Purple

188 1985. Challenging the deportation order served on a Lutheran priest.
Silkscreened poster produced for Lutheran Youth at CAP, Cape Town
Red

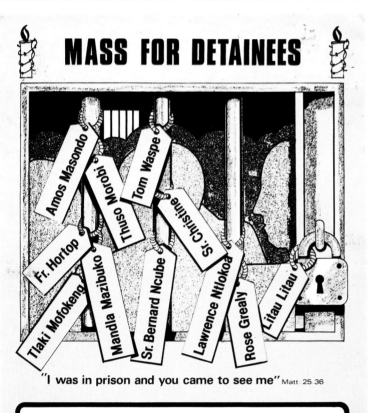

189 1986. Catholic Church bears witness for Christians in detention.
Offset litho poster produced by the Catholic Diocese of Johannesburg
Black and yellow

Each one, teach one...

Education

Each one, teach one...

On 16 June 1976 secondary school students of Soweto decided that they would not submit to the imposition of Afrikaans as a medium of instruction. They had also had enough of racist and inferior education. Under the banner of the 'Action Committee' of the South African Students Movement (SASM) pupils organised a protest march. Groups from the different Soweto schools gathered and moved towards Orlando stadium to hold a mass meeting. Units of the South African Police moved in swiftly, firing live ammunition. This protest and the resulting deaths marked the beginning of an uprising which spread rapidly throughout South Africa; hundreds of school students were killed. Education had become a terrain of violence, and has remained so.

Segregated schooling has been fundamental to apartheid education policy. When the white Nationalist government steered the Bantu Education Act through parliament in 1953/1954, their intentions were clear:

> I will reform education so that Natives will be taught from childhood that equality with Europeans is not for them.
> *(Hendrik Verwoerd)*

> We should not give the Natives any academic education. If we do, who is going to do the manual labour in the community?
> *(JN le Roux)*

The events of 1976 were not merely local protests against inadequate schooling. The uprising spread so rapidly throughout the country precisely because it was directed at an educational and political dispensation which had oppressed black people for over a quarter of a century.

The commemoration of 16 June became a central focus of resistance in student and youth politics in South Africa. The youth of the 1980s, the 'young lions' of the townships as they dubbed themselves, forged their political consciousness in the schools of the post-1976 period. By 1985, 16 June had become a *de facto* public holiday, reluctantly called Soweto Day by the white establishment, and officially proclaimed South African Youth Day by the liberation movement inside and outside the country. The posters of the 1980s continually affirm the significance of this day for students and youth throughout the country.

In strategic terms, the events of 1976 brought to the fore the central contradiction which was to shape and dominate educational politics in the 1980s: this was the conflict between the inferior education provided in separate schools for black children by the state, and the progressive education demanded by, and increasingly practised by, organised students, parents and teachers.

The Congress of South African Students (COSAS) was formed in 1979. It was to become the largest mass-based student organisation South Africa had ever seen. By August 1985, when COSAS was banned by government decree, it had mobilised a support-base of hundreds of thousands of secondary school students spread across 71 branches nationwide. There is no doubt that COSAS played a significant role in the period from 1980 to 1985: its networks, organisational structures and the popular support it commanded politicised many thousands of people, carrying the message of national democratic struggle into townships everywhere.

On the education front, COSAS's programme of action sought to achieve dynamic, free and compulsory education for all. The organisation was in the forefront of educational protest, consistently demanding the abolition of the harshest features of black education – inferior and segregated schooling, poor facilities, textbook shortages, exclusions of students for political reasons, age limits, corporal punishment, sexual harassment and the like.

COSAS was the driving force behind mass educational struggles of the first half of the 1980s, but other organisations also made important contributions to the democratic movement in this period. Two of the most prominent were the National Union of South African Students (NUSAS), and the Azanian Students Organisation (AZASO), which was later to change its name to the South African National Students Congress (SANSCO).

AZASO concentrated on organising black students at tertiary institutions, and established branches at universities, teacher-training colleges and technikons throughout the country.

AZASO structures were pivotal to student resistance on black campuses. They highlighted the authoritarian educational practices and apartheid-oriented curriculae which characterised these institutions. On the mainly-white campuses such as the University of the Witwatersrand (Wits) and the University of Cape Town (UCT), AZASO powerfully articulated the grievances of black students who experienced particular difficulties and inequalities at these institutions.

NUSAS concentrated most of its energies on winning the active support of white students at English-medium universities. In recent years, however, it has managed to establish a presence on some Afrikaans campuses as well. NUSAS campaigns tended to focus on bringing struggles of the factories, townships and rural areas onto campus. It advocated the need for a less eurocentric and more politically critical content in university courses in all faculties. Much of the media and other propaganda produced had an impact far beyond NUSAS, as it was often used in educational activities of other organisations such as COSAS and AZASO.

Most activities undertaken by COSAS, AZASO and NUSAS were reactive, and characterised by protest action. However, the Education Charter campaign taken up by these three organisations in February 1984 actively expressed a need – widely recognised by student leaders at the time – to formulate concrete alternatives to apartheid education. During 1984 and early 1985 all three student organisations worked hard at popularising a campaign to draw up an Education Charter. By the end of 1984, the progressive teachers' union, the National Education Union of South Africa (NEUSA), had joined the alliance.

The Education Charter was conceived of as an elaboration of the Freedom Charter's assertion that 'the doors of learning and culture shall be opened'. It aimed to put forward a detailed view of a viable alternative to apartheid education. A specific aim of the Education Charter campaign was the creation of a document around which students could organise.

When it joined the Education Charter campaign, NEUSA was relatively small. In the early 1980s it ran subject workshops for teachers and built programmatic alliances with student organisations. By 1985 significant numbers of teachers throughout the country began to actively identify with the anti-apartheid struggle. NEUSA experienced a rapid growth in membership in the Eastern Cape, Transvaal and Natal, and similar progressive teacher associations were launched in the Western Cape – the Western Cape Teachers Union (WECTU), and the Democratic Teachers Union (DETU) – and in the Border Region the East London Progressive Teachers Union (ELPTU).

Despite these developments, a serious impasse arose during 1985 in the struggle against apartheid education. Student organisations had come to rely too heavily on the boycott tactic. Schooling was at a standstill. While this was testimony to COSAS's political power, it dispersed students onto the streets and made further, more constructive organisation virtually impossible.

The declaration of a State of Emergency in July 1985 and the subsequent banning of COSAS only served to exacerbate the problem. There was talk of 1986 being a year of no schooling. Many students spoke naively of 'liberation before education', which caused widespread alarm in the townships.

During September, representatives of all sections of the Soweto community met to discuss possible solutions to the growing education crisis in the township. They formed the Soweto Parents Crisis Committee (SPCC), which represented a new form of political organisation in the education terrain. For the first time ever, an alliance of parents, teachers and students was established to tackle problems in education. The SPCC achieved widespread support throughout Soweto, and the establishment of parent-teacher-student alliances was soon on the national agenda.

With this in mind, an historic national education conference was convened in Johannesburg in December 1985. The National Education Crisis Committee (NECC) was launched at this conference. It adopted the slogan 'People's Education for People's Power' to express the strategic objective of future educational struggle. The conference resolved to call on students to return to school immediately, while continuing the struggle for proper education.

At a later conference, held in March 1986 in Durban, this call was reiterated, with a resolution that people's education programmes should be implemented immediately.

Progressive educational organisations have successfully drawn attention to the problems of education in South Africa, and have made significant contributions to the process of working out possible solutions. But the black education system remains in crisis.

A recent government report proposes compulsory primary school education for children of all races, but retains existing apartheid-created inequalities in teaching and resources, within a supposedly non-racial framework. Indeed, rather than open up under-utilised white schools to relieve over-crowded and dilapidated township schools, the government plans to close them down. The government continues to evade taking the only rational course – that of integrating education – by developing elaborate procedures for modifying the present system.

Meanwhile, hundreds of thousands of black children continue to receive inadequate education with few prospects. ❏

90 1986. The UDF commemorates the tenth anniversary of Soweto Day, 16 June, when Soweto students rose up against bantu education and the system of apartheid.

Offset litho poster produced by STP for the UDF, Transvaal
Black, red and yellow

191 1987. Celebrating the youth–worker alliance and commemorating 16 June. The language used is Zulu. (Many COSATU posters were produced in Zulu, Sotho and English)
Offset litho poster produced by COSATU, Johannesburg
Black, red and yellow

192 1984. Youth and students reaffirm their determination to fight until victory is achieved.
Silkscreened poster produced by AYCO and COSAS at STP, Johannesburg
Black

193 1984. The Alexander Youth Congress held a printing workshop at its annual general meeting; one of the posters produced marked the death of Hector Peterson, the first person to die in the Soweto uprising of 1976. (Note the police confiscation signature in the bottom right hand corner)
Silkscreened poster produced by AYCO at an STP workshop in Johannesburg
Red

194 c1986. The people of Kagiso, a township next to Krugersdorp near Johannesburg, remember 16 June..
Spray painted poster produced by Kagiso youth
Red and black

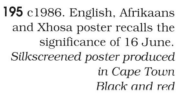

195 c1986. English, Afrikaans and Xhosa poster recalls the significance of 16 June.
Silkscreened poster produced in Cape Town
Black and red

196 c1987. A joint UDF and COSATU stayaway on 16 June commemorates the death of Hector Peterson and others in 1976.
Offset litho poster produced by the UDF and COSATU, Cape Town
Black, red and yellow

197 1986. A prayer meeting to observe 16 June.
Offset litho poster produced by the WPCC, Cape Town
Black and red

198 1987. Militant township youths demand people's education rather than gutter education, and that June 1976 not be forgotten.
Silkscreened poster produced at CAP by CAYCO Townships, Cape Peninsula
Red

REMEMBER
JUNE 16 1976

1976 was a year of tears, a year of blood and death – but it was also a turning point in our determined struggle.

It was a moment of truth when students stood up for their rights. They braved the heavy hand of apartheid to demand democracy in education.

Today we now see mass action not only by students, but also by youth, workers, residents and women. We see hundreds of people's organisations taking root. We see civic bodies, trade unions, residents organisations, and student and youth groups.

Many of these organisations have come together under the banner of the United Democratic Front – the UDF. They have united the struggles for democracy in the schools, the townships, at work and in the government.

United action is now the order of the day.

Despite all efforts by the racist government to fool us, our suffering has not changed since 1976. Our spirit of our struggle has also not changed over this time. What has changed is that today we are organised and stronger. Today, freedom is nearer.

FROM MOBILISATION TO ORGANISATION!
LONG LIVE THE STRUGGLE FOR DEMOCRACY!

199 1985. Paying homage to the struggle of 16 June and celebrating organisation and unity under the banner of the UDF.
Offset litho poster produced by STP for the UDF, Johannesburg
Black, red and yellow

200 1985. The call for a democratic education system.
Silkscreened poster produced at a training workshop at STP, Johannesburg
Black, yellow and red

201 1985. COSAS uses the occasion of 16 June to emphasise the Freedom Charter's call for an open education system and the demand for the SADF to leave the townships – shortly after this poster was produced, COSAS was banned.
Offset litho poster produced for COSAS by STP, Johannesburg
Black

202 1985. The face in the upper right-hand corner is of a student killed in 1984.
Silkscreened poster produced by COSAS at STP, Johannesburg
Black

203 1985. COSAS announces the launch of a cultural committee in a local branch.
Silkscreened poster produced by COSAS Wentworth branch, Natal
Black

204 1986. An anti-military 'jorl' (party)
for school pupils in the white
areas of Johannesburg.
*Silkscreened poster produced by ECC at
STP, Johannesburg
Red*

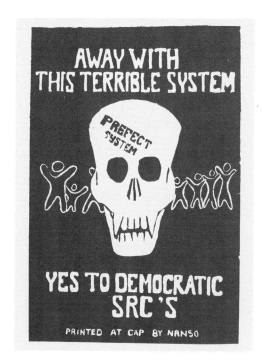

205 1985. Students in occupied
Namibia echo the demands made by
students in South Africa.
*Silkscreened poster produced by
NANSO at CAP, Cape Town
Red*

206 1985. Namibian students demand an end to Afrikaans as the medium of instruction at schools.
Silkscreened poster produced by NANSO at CAP in Cape Town
Blue

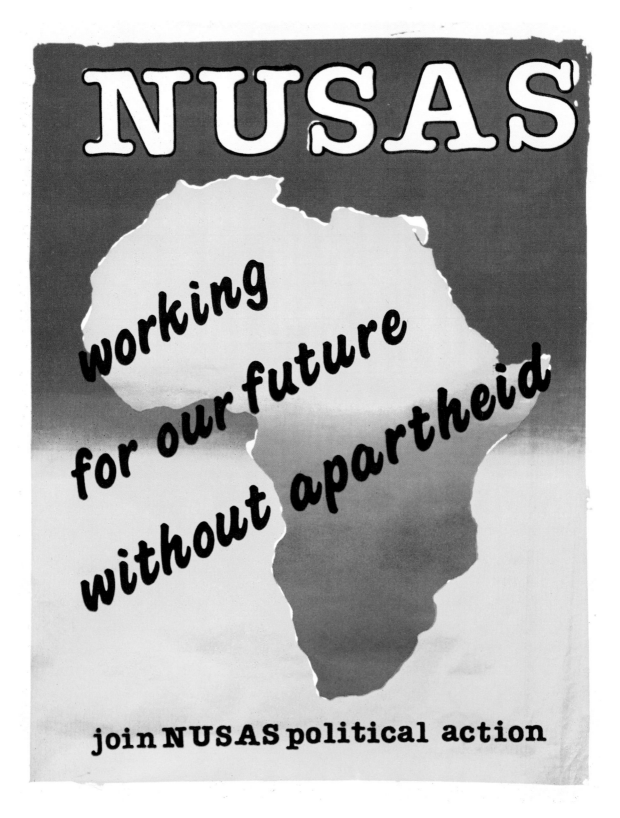

207 1987. Announcing a NUSAS national campaign.
Silkscreened poster produced by NUSAS, University of the Witwatersrand, Johannesburg
Black, red, yellow and blue (marbled)

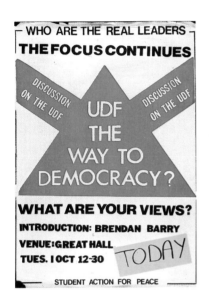

208 1985. Advertising a student campaign debate.
Silkscreened poster produced by Projects Committee, Wits, Johannesburg
Black and green

209 1985. Advertising a student campaign debate.
Silkscreened poster produced by Projects Committee, Wits, Johannesburg
Black and yellow

210 1985. Cultural event to promote people's education.
Silkscreened poster produced by AZASO at CAP, Cape Town
Black, green and yellow

The streets of our country are in turmoil. The universities are filled with students rioting and rebelling. Communists seek to destroy our country. Russia is threatening us with her might and the Republic is in danger from within and without.

We need Law and Order! Without it our Nation cannot survive.

Adolf Hitler 1932

MAKES YOU THINK DOESN'T IT?

A National NUSAS Campaign

211 1985. NUSAS campaign poster quotes Hitler as a comment on South Africa.
Offset litho poster produced by NUSAS, Cape Town
Black, green and pink

212 1985. NUSAS comments on the impact that President PW Botha and Law and Order Minister Louis le Grange had on South African society.
Offset litho poster produced by NUSAS, Cape Town
Black, yellow and pink

213 1989. Poster by the Black Students Interim Committee (BSIC), set up at Wits in 1989 after the Black Students Society (BSS) was banned.
Silkscreened poster produced by BSIC, Wits, Johannesburg
Black and red on yellow card

214 1985. NUSAS celebrates May Day.
Offset litho poster produced by NUSAS, Cape Town
Black, red and yellow

NATIONAL EDUCATION CONFERENCE

Peoples' Education for Peoples' Power!

Durban, 29/30 March '86

Issued by: NATIONAL EDUCATION CRISIS COMMITTEE, C o 318 West Walk, Dbn. - Printed by ART PRINTERS - 73 Beatrice St., Dbn.

215 1986. Conference held to address the education crisis in black schools at a time when students were boycotting around the country.
Offset litho poster produced by NECC, Johannesburg
Black, red and yellow

216 1985. Students take control of the destiny of their schools.
Silkscreened poster produced by Education Crisis Committee at CAP, Cape Town
Red

217 1984. The launch of a joint campaign by COSAS, NUSAS, NEUSA and AZASO for an Education Charter.
Silkscreened poster produced by the Education Charter Campaign Committee, Transvaal, at STP, Johannesburg
Blue

218 1987. A call for the police and SADF to stay out of the schools.
Offset litho poster produced by Free the Children's Alliance and NECC, Cape Town
Black

219 1985. NEUSA meets to discuss the crisis in black education.
Silkscreened poster produced by NEUSA, Johannesburg at STP, Johannesburg
Black and blue

220 1986. A comment on the anti-education effects of Christian National Education, radio and TV.
Silkscreened poster produced by EDASA at CAP, Cape Town
Black and red

221 1986. Teachers' union demands that the state stop harassment of teachers.
Silkscreened poster produced by WECTU, Cape Town
Black and yellow

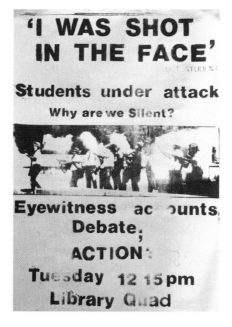

222 c1985. University of Cape Town meets to discuss police violence against students.
Silkscreened poster produced by UCT students, Cape Town
Red

223 c1985. A call on students to become involved in the affairs of their society.
Silkscreened poster produced by Projects Committee, Wits, Johannesburg
Black and yellow

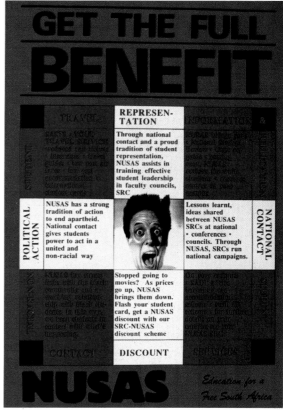

224 c1985. Conscientising poster on suppression of information through censorship.
Silkscreened poster produced by NUSAS
Black and blue

225 1987. Setting out the many ways in which NUSAS plays a role in the lives of university students.
Offset litho poster produced by NUSAS
Black, red and blue

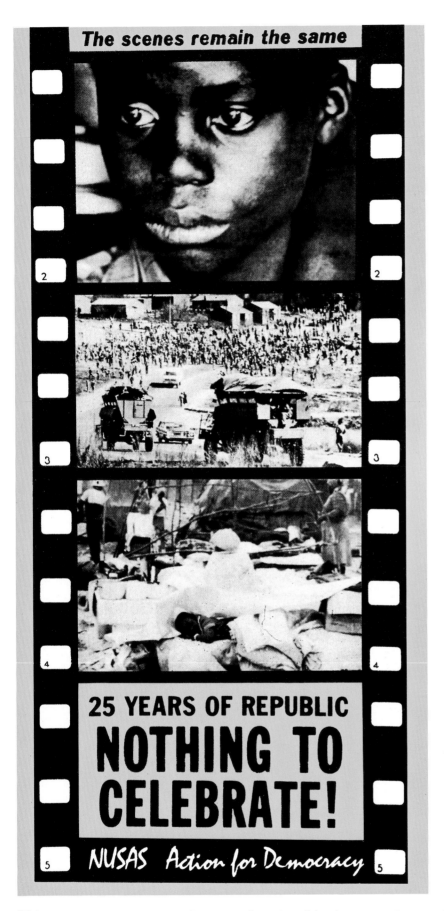

226 1986. NUSAS notes that there is nothing to celebrate
after 25 years of a white racist republic.
Offset litho poster produced by NUSAS, Cape Town
Black and yellow

Siyaya noba kubi

Militarisation and Repression

We will continue, despite the hardships

During the 1980s, repression was rife throughout South Africa: in education, with children controlled on their school grounds by security forces; in political life, with political organisations banned and restricted; in the workplace, with labour laws aimed at limiting union activity; in community life, where people protesting against issues such as rent increases were shot down in cold blood; in the media; in cultural life; in the churches and in the courts. Thousands of political activists, unionists, youth and school children risked harassment, long periods of detention without trial, and even death at the hands of the apartheid state.

To prop up the apartheid system the Nationalist government introduced stringent security laws, which increased in harshness and sophistication over the decades. Legislation gave the state wide powers to detain opponents without trial, and to ban people, organisations, gatherings and publications. Under these laws, people could be held in prison for interrogation, as potential witnesses for the state, or as a 'preventative measure'. Access to lawyers and family could be denied and detainees could be kept in solitary confinement indefinitely. Detainees had little if any protection, and many detainees testified to torture and assault. (Security legislation was modified in 1991 to remove many of its most repressive measures.) Over 70 people have died in detention since 1963. (Statistics provided by the Human Rights Commission.)

During the States of Emergency from 1985 to 1990, the state granted itself even further-ranging powers of detention. Over 52 000 people were detained during this time, some of them for three consecutive years. Over 25% of those detained were children, and at times a far higher percentage of detainees were minors.

Ironically, detainees were themselves instrumental in exerting pressure for their release. At the beginning of 1989, one group of long-term detainees after another went on hunger strike, vowing to fast to the death if necessary. With the outside world watching, they gained their freedom one by one, although most were released under severe restrictions.

The releases did not stop the system of detention without trial But they did lead to the nationwide Defiance Campaign of 1989, in which the Mass Democratic Movement mobilised increasingly effective pressure for change.

Emergency regulations virtually outlawed any form of political activity that might challenge the state. Thirty-two organisations were effectively banned in 1988; boycott actions were prohibited; protest campaigns were forbidden. Police, using teargas, sjamboks, birdshot, rubber bullets and live ammunition continually broke up marches and demonstrations; authorities often proscribed funerals, dictating when and where they could be held and how many mourners could attend. Meetings and conferences were banned, and newspapers closed down for months on end.

The law was used with explicitly repressive intent. Political trials were employed to hamstring democratic leaders, with one central figure after another getting caught up in the snares of treason trials running for months, sometimes years. Bail was usually denied. Many leaders were found not guilty, after years in prison awaiting trial.

Many thousands of people engaging in marches and demonstrations, including children, were arrested and charged with criminal offences. Relatively few cases actually resulted in convictions, but when sentences were imposed they were harsh. The application of the doctrine of common purpose is an example, as in the case of the 'Sharpeville Six'. This group was sentenced to death on the basis that they had formed part of a group which was present at the killing of a community councillor. The sentence was later commuted to life imprisonment after the moratorium on the death penalty in February 1991. By mid-1991 some of this group had been released.

South Africa also has one of the worst records in the world for capital punishment – 627 prisoners were executed in the five years from 1983 to 1987. But apartheid's legal repressive structures have been increasingly underpinned by more sinister covert forces such as hit-squads, within the country and beyond our borders. Their actions range from irritating harassment to the cold-blooded murder of individuals and groups: their activities include smear pamphlets, bomb threats, slashed vehicle tyres, dead animals on the doorsteps of activists' homes, bricks or teargas canisters thrown into homes or offices, arson, burglaries, kidnapping and assassination. These hit-squads, operating from within the police, the army and local government structures, appear to be badly controlled and ill-informed, but well-armed and well-protected against exposure. They appear to have been responsible for over 50 assassinations of political activists since 1977.

Vigilante groups have also been covertly and overtly supported by security forces against communities resisting local authorities. They have been used particularly brutally in the bantustans and in rural Natal, but also in urban communities.

Thousands of people have died in this violence over the last five years; recent evidence has implicated the security forces directly in its instigation and in actual attacks.

From 1986 onwards, the state co-ordinated its repressive strategy through the National Security Management System. This structure, presided over by the State Security Council consisting of cabinet ministers and senior military and police officers, formed a countrywide network of Joint Management Centres (JMCs) made up of security police, army personnel and invited members of local government and community. JMCs gathered information on organisations and local activists, attempted to counteract their activities by various means, and co-ordinated local security forces. Evidence also links them to hit-squads and vigilante activities.

The cost of the struggle for real democracy in South Africa has been high. Thousands of lives have been ruined, thousands have been killed. Armed with immense legislative and military powers, the authorities have not flinched from crushing opposition. Where the law has not sufficed, they have stepped outside it with monstrous brutality and the arrogance of the unaccountable.

The End Conscription Campaign

At the end of the 1960s, compulsory military conscription for all white males was introduced in South Africa. The apartheid government needed an army ready and prepared to defend its policies against resistance both inside the country and across its borders. Until 1983, opposition to conscription was muted and limited. But late that year, the Black Sash civil liberties group publicly called for an end to compulsory conscription and in response, the End Conscription Campaign (ECC) was formed. Its central demand was for the right of conscripts to choose not to serve in the South African Defence Force (SADF).

The ECC was established as a coalition of many human rights, student, religious and women's groups, all opposed to conscription and militarisation, and committed to working for a just peace in South Africa. The organisation campaigned around the fundamental belief that no person should be forced either to take up arms, or to take life. In South Africa, this stand was specifically linked to the role the SADF played in the townships within the country and in neighbouring states.

The ECC argued that the SADF's primary role should be to serve the interests of all South Africans. Instead, it was being used to defend the system of apartheid against the legitimate aspirations of the majority of South Africa's people, as well as those of the people of Namibia and the rest of Southern Africa.

The ECC identified itself with the cause of the oppressed and sought to contribute to the struggle for liberation. It called for the withdrawal of the SADF from Namibia, Angola and South Africa's townships, for an end to the increasing militarisation of all aspects of South African society, for conscientious objectors to have the right to do alternative national service, and for a just peace in South Africa.

Conscription directly affected the white population, giving the ECC a different constituency from most anti-apartheid groups. It therefore had to use new tactics. Conventional political activities like mass meetings, seminars and press conferences were complemented by fun runs, fairs, kite-flying and street theatre. There were cultural events like rock concerts, art exhibitions, film festivals and cabaret. Tens of thousands of colourful stickers, T-shirts, posters and pamphlets were produced. Strong campaigns of support for jailed objectors were mounted.

This dynamic style of campaigning allowed a broad range of people to express their unhappiness with conscription – parents whose sons faced call-ups, school and university students, English-speaking churches, radical Afrikaners, and artists, musicians and actors.

By working among whites against two crucial aspects of the maintenance of apartheid – conscription and the SADF – the ECC won acclaim in the black community, which saw ECC campaigns as contributing to building non-racialism. ECC co-operated closely with mass organisations such as the United Democratic Front and its affiliates, and undertook community upliftment projects in black areas to demonstrate solidarity with township residents.

The government accused the ECC of being a 'communist', 'subversive' organisation contributing to the 'revolutionary onslaught' against South Africa by undermining the army and encouraging conscripts to disobey their call-ups. By the mid-1980s, the ECC was experiencing an endless stream of state harassment. Its meetings and publications were banned, its activists were detained without trial or subjected to intense harassment, and its offices were raided by security police. In 1988, it was restricted.

This repression in no way dampened the ECC's spirit, however. Today it still mounts campaigns against compulsory military service and has done much to assist exiles returning after the unbanning of the ANC and other organisations on 2 February 1990. ❏

228 1984. A sinister figure masked with the colours of the South African flag symbolises what ECC has fought against.
Offset litho poster produced by ECC, Cape Town
Black, blue and orange

227 1986. Poster using Picasso's 'Guernica', created to express his anguish at the Spanish Civil War, as a means of bringing home the horror of civil strife in South Africa.
Offset litho poster produced by ECC, Johannesburg
Black and red

229 1985. ECC condemns conscription and social injustice.
Silkscreened poster produced by ECC at STP, Johannesburg
Red, green, yellow and black

230 1986. Outlining basic demands that would be met in a peaceful society.
Silkscreened poster produced by ECC at STP, Johannesburg
Blue

231 1986. Bilingual poster calling for an end to national service.
Silkscreened poster produced by ECC at STP, Johannesburg
Black and red

232 1986. Conscripts demand the right not to serve in the SADF.
Offset litho poster produced by ECC, Cape Town
Black

233 1985. A warning is sounded about the long-term implications of cadet training in schools.
(Hey man – didn't they tell you? Cadets makes you mad)
Silkscreened poster produced by ECC at CAP, Cape Town
Black, red and yellow

BOTHA EK'S GATVOL

End Conscription Campaign

234 1987. Anger grows against conscription. (Botha, I'm fed up) *Offset litho poster produced by ECC, Johannesburg Sepia*

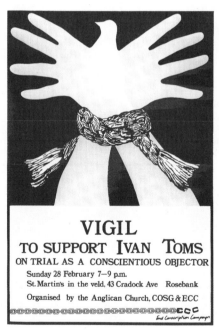

VIGIL
TO SUPPORT IVAN TOMS
ON TRIAL AS A CONSCIENTIOUS OBJECTOR
Sunday 28 February 7—9 p.m.
St. Martin's in the veld, 43 Cradock Ave Rosebank
Organised by the Anglican Church, COSG & ECC

End Conscription Campaign

235 1987. Vigil to support Ivan Toms, on trial as a conscientious objector. *Offset litho poster produced by ECC, Johannesburg Black and flesh colour*

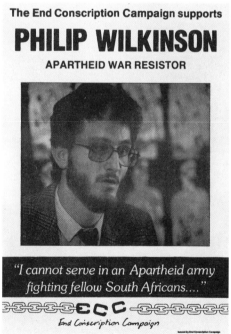

The End Conscription Campaign supports

PHILIP WILKINSON

APARTHEID WAR RESISTOR

"I cannot serve in an Apartheid army fighting fellow South Africans...."

End Conscription Campaign

236 1986. Support for conscientious objector Philip Wilkinson. *Offset litho produced by ECC, Johannesburg Black*

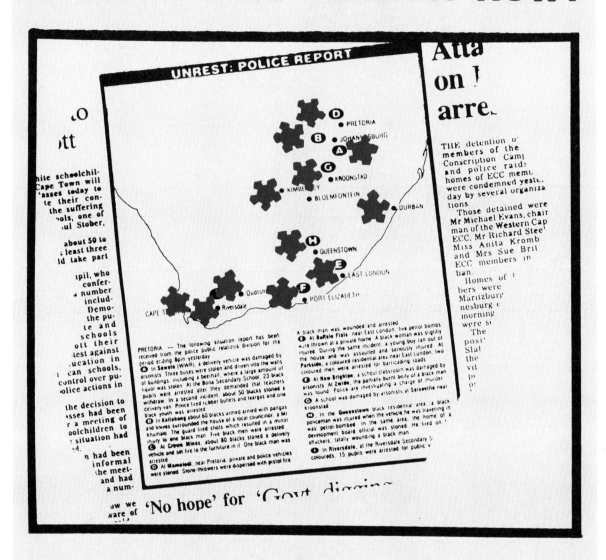

237 1985. Why are troops, conscripted to fight on the border against SA's enemies, deployed in townships inside the country?
Silkscreened poster produced by ECC at CAP, Cape Town
Black and red

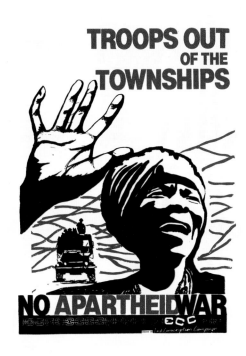

238 1984. Protesting the presence of troops in the townships.
Silkscreened poster produced by ECC at STP, Johannesburg
Black and red

239 1985. Denouncing the SADF's occupation of Crossroads.
Silkscreened poster produced by ECC at CAP, Cape Town
Black and red

240 1987. What are you looking for in the townships, soldier?
Silkscreened poster produced by ECC, Johannesburg
Black

241 1986. Condemning the presence of the SADF in schools.
Silkscreened poster produced by ECC, Johannesburg
Black and yellow

242 1987. Anti-conscription forces
protest SADF destruction of
Namibian schools.
*Silkscreened poster produced by
NANSO and printed at CAP,
Cape Town
Black*

243 1988. Advertising an
information meeting on Angola.
*Poster produced by ECC,
Johannesburg
Black*

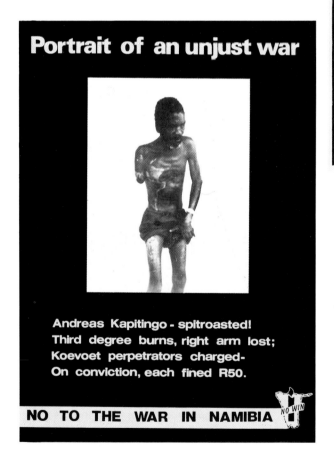

244 1984. Exposing the atrocities of the
Namibian war – part of a series used at guerilla
theatre in shopping centres in the Western Cape.
Most of the activists involved were arrested.
*Offset litho poster produced by SUCA, Cape Town
Black*

245 1984. Protesting SADF's
role in Namibia, and pointing
out parallels with the USA's
involvement in Vietnam.
*Silkscreened poster produced
by ECC, Johannesburg
Black and red*

246 1984. Peace poster calling for the removal of SADF troops from Namibia.
Silkscreened poster produced by ECC at STP, Johannesburg
Black and red

GABERONE

THE KILLING CONTINUES

MASS MEETING
Sunday 23 June 3 pm
St George's Church Silvertown

247 1985. Mass meeting decries assassinations by SADF in Gaborone, Botswana.
Silkscreened poster produced for UDF by CAP, Cape Town
Brown

SADF HANDS OFF OUR NEIGHBOURS

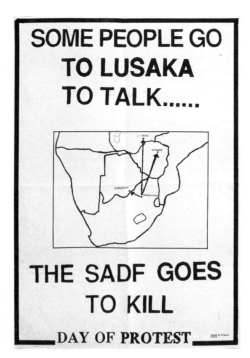

SOME PEOPLE GO
TO LUSAKA
TO TALK......

THE SADF GOES
TO KILL

DAY OF PROTEST

248 1985. Call for day of protest over SADF killings in Lusaka, and highlighting talks between the ANC and others from the business community to student groupings.
Silkscreened poster produced by Projects Committee, Wits, Johannesburg
Black

249 1985. The SADF is told to keep out of neighbouring states.
Silkscreened poster
Black

250 1986. Demanding an end to SADF raids into neighbouring countries.
Offset litho poster produced by ECC, Johannesburg
Black and red

251 1986. Commemorating death of Mozambican president Samora Machel.
Offset litho poster produced for UDF, Johannesburg
Black, red and yellow

252 1989. Announcing a meeting to protest the State of Emergency.
Offset litho poster produced by TOPS for WAR, Johannesburg
Black and green

253 1987. A call to use Christmas as a time to protest against the State of Emergency and the detention of thousands of children.
Offset litho poster produced by the UDF for Campaign for National United Action, Johannesburg
Black

254 1985. Raising awareness of death squads.
Offset litho poster produced for JODAC, ECC, NEUSA, DESCOM and DPSC by STP, Johannesburg
Black and red

255 1986. Protesting the introduction by the then Minister of Law and Order of laws further suppressing democratic rights.
Silkscreened poster produced by DESCOM, Johannesburg
Black and red

BOTHA'S EMERGENCY

REGULATIONS IN TERMS OF THE PUBLIC SAFETY
ACT, 1953

256 1985. The UDF expresses opposition to the State of Emergency and the repressive actions of SADF troops in the townships.
Silkscreened poster produced by UDF at CAP, Cape Town
Black and red

257 1985. Eastern Cape community leaders Matthew Goniwe, Fort Calata, Sicelo Mhlawuli and Sparrow Mkhonto were assassinated by 'unknown persons'.
Offset litho poster produced by SASPU National, Johannesburg
Black and red

SIPHIWO MTIMKULU STUDENT LEADER

DETAINED. POISONED. MISSING.

COMMEMORATION SERVICE

BRIAN MBULELO MAZIBUKO

WE STILL REMEMBER YOU COMRADE

14 OCT 1984 10.30 A.M. MATHOLE CINEMA

Issued by Moya youth movement ((Tembisa))

258 c1985. Siphiwe Mtimkulu disappeared after alleging that he was poisoned by police while in detention – he is still missing.
Offset litho poster produced by Media Committee, University of Cape Town
Black

259 1984. Youth group commemorates the death of activist Brian Mbulelo Mazibuko.
Silkscreened poster produced by Moya Youth Movement (Tembisa) at STP, Johannesburg
Blue

HAMBANI KAHLE MA-COMRADES

PHINEAS SIBIYA

FLORENCE MNIKATHI

SIMON NGUBANE

ALPHEUS NKABINDE

ASISOZE SANILIBALA FUTHI SIYOQHUBEKA NJALO NOMZABALAZO ENAWUFELA

MAWU

We will never forget you, we will never give up the cause you died for

Issued by MAWU · P O Box 18106 Dalbridge
Printed by ART PRINTERS - Dbn.

260 1986. MAWU commemorates the assassination of four unionists.
Offset litho poster produced by MAWU
Black and red

DAVID WEBSTER

fought for democracy murdered by apartheid

Issued by the David Webster Funeral Committee, P O Box 32723, Braamfontein 2017

261 1989. Human rights activist David Webster was assassinated outside his home on May Day 1989.
Offset litho poster produced by the David Webster Funeral Committee
Black

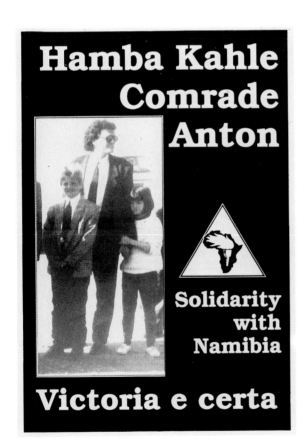

262 1989. Anton Lubowski, a leading SWAPO member, was assassinated during the run-up to Namibian independence.
Offset litho poster produced by Namibia Solidarity Committee, South Africa
Black

263 1989. Jabu Ndlovu, a NUMSA official, was killed at her home after returning from a national NUMSA meeting.
Offset litho poster produced by NUMSA
Black, red, blue and yellow

264 1985. Nineteen people were massacred by police during a march in Langa, outside Uitenhage.
Offset litho poster produced for UDF at CAP
Black

265 1985. Demanding an end to the killings in the Vaal and East Rand townships.
Silkscreened poster produced by Vaal youth at STP, Johannesburg
Red

266 1985. Queenstown in the Northern Cape was the scene of one of the many massacres of anti-apartheid activists in a confrontation with the army and police.
Offset litho poster produced for the Queenstown community at STP, Johannesburg
Black and red

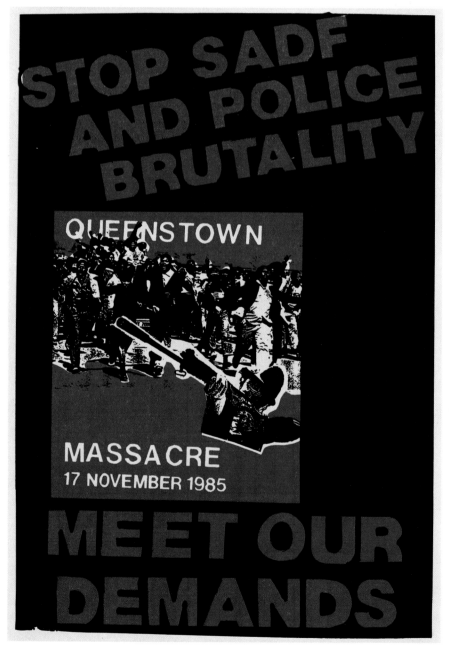

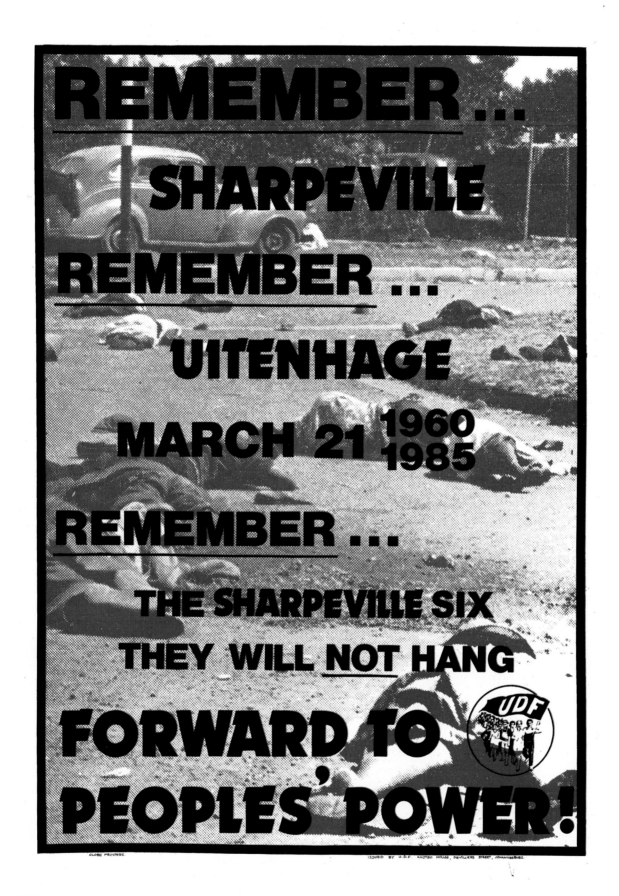

267 1985. The massacres in Sharpeville and Uitenhage
both took place on 21 March, although 25 years apart.
Offset litho poster produced for the UDF by STP, Johannesburg
Black and red

268 1986. Honouring the four Cradock
community leaders assassinated
the previous year.
*Offset litho poster produced by the UDF
at CAP, Cape Town*
Red

269 1986. A rally in Alexandra following
a police massacre of residents in the
township by police.
Offset litho poster
Black

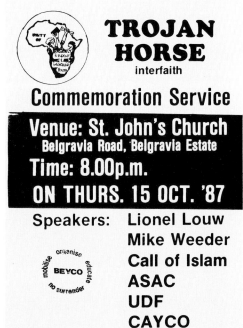

270 1987. In the Trojan Horse incident
police hidden on the back of a truck
drove past protesters and opened fire,
killing a number of children.
*Offset litho poster produced by BEYCO,
Cape Town*
Black and yellow

271 1986. The people cry out.
Silkscreened poster produced at STP
Red

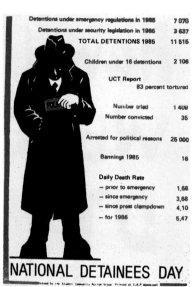

272 1985. Observing National Detainees Day.
Silkscreened poster produced by ADAC at CAP, Cape Town Blue, brown, red and yellow

Detentions under emergency regulations in 1985	7 070
Detentions under security legislation in 1985	3 637
TOTAL DETENTIONS 1985	**11 515**
Children under 16 detentions	2 106
UCT Report 83 percent tortured	
Number tried	1 409
Number convicted	35
Arrested for political reasons	25 000
Bannings 1985	16
Daily Death Rate	
— prior to emergency	1,68
— since emergency	3,68
— since press clampdown	4,10
— for 1986	5,47

NATIONAL DETAINEES DAY

273 1986. National Detainees Day poster.
Silkscreened poster produced by the Students Community Action Group at CAP Black and red

RELEASE OUR PEOPLE

RALLY
REV McCAMEL'S TEMPLE
EVATON
24 March
2pm
speakers:
SAMSON NDOU AMANDA KWADI COSAS

ISSUED BY DESCOM,DPSC,UDF. KHOTSO HOUSE,DE VILLIERS ST,JHB.

274 1985. 'Release our people' rally in Evaton, a Vaal Triangle township.
Offset litho poster produced by DESCOM, DPSC and UDF Black and red

JUNE 1 1987 INTERNATIONAL CHILDREN'S DAY **IN SOUTH AFRICA MORE THAN 1400 CHILDREN ARE AT PRESENT BEING HELD IN DETENTION**

275 1987. International Children's Day poster protests against the number of children in South African prisons.
Silkscreened poster produced by Molo Songololo at CAP, Cape Town Black

276 1989. Demanding the lifting of the State of Emergency
and the release of all detainees following a widespread hunger strike.
Offset litho poster produced by the Hunger Strikers' Committee
Black and yellow

COMRADE

PETER NCHABELENG

PRESIDENT ~ UDF N. TRANSVAAL

A COMBATANT FOR LIFE

A PATRIOT TO THE END

Globe.

Issued by UDF, Khotso House, Johannesburg.

277 1986. Comrade Peter Nchabeleng, a stalwart of the struggle, died in detention.
Offset litho poster produced by MARS for UDF, Johannesburg
Black, red and yellow

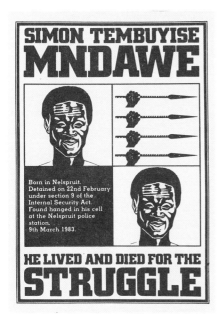

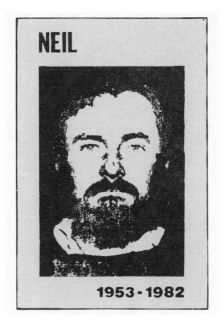

278 1983. Simon Tembuyise Mndawe, found hanged in his detention cell.
Offset litho poster
Black

279 1984. Commemorating the 1982 death in detention of unionist Neil Aggett.
Silkscreened poster produced by STP, Johannesburg
Black and blue

> But who killed Neil, mama. . . ?
> Ssssssssshhh! sleep and grow strong.
> Who, mama. . . ?
> His own clothing, that's what was blamed.
> So thula, thula, now quiet my child.
>
> Jeremy Cronin   1984

280 1984. Verse from a poem about death in detention.
Silkscreened poster produced by STP, Johannesburg
Black

281 1982. Poster used in the motorcade protest held after Neil Aggett's death.
Stencilled poster
Black

282 1986. The Sharpeville Six were sentenced to death for a political killing under the 'common purpose' doctrine; they were eventually reprieved, but given long jail sentences.
Offset litho poster produced by the UDF
Black and red on yellow paper

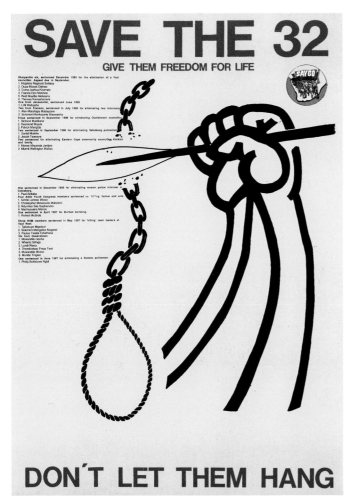

SAVE THE 32
GIVE THEM FREEDOM FOR LIFE

283 1988. Many political prisoners were sentenced to death.
Offset litho poster produced for SAYCO by Graphic Equalizer Black, red and yellow

DON'T LET THEM HANG

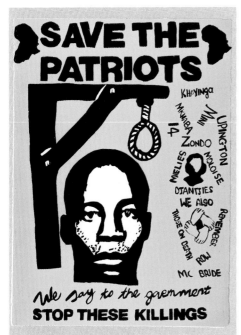

284 1988. Demanding an end to the proposed hangings of a number of political prisoners.
Silkscreened poster Black and yellow

285 1986. Opposing the death sentence imposed on one of the Sharpeville Six.
Silkscreened poster produced by CAYCO at CAP, Cape Town Black

The doors of culture shall be opened!

Culture

The doors of culture shall be opened!

The grassroots political mobilisation of the 1980s sparked off a massive surge in 'people's culture'. As people found the political voice to shout out their angers, beliefs, griefs and victories, they learned to express these also in cultural forms – from toyi-toyi to jazz, from poster-making to workers' theatre and oral poetry. Youth, women, workers, students and conscientious objectors began to create the image of a people with dignity, of a community striving for the values of non-racialism, democracy and an end to economic oppression.

Apartheid culture vs people's culture

Apartheid society has, over the decades, severely distorted the practise and perception of culture. 'Culture' was used to justify colonialism, with claims that European civilisation was better, that African societies were 'barbarous' and 'savage'. In South Africa, this remained a basic presumption. Apartheid law also divided the black population into 'ethnic groups', supposedly based on pre-colonial kingdoms and cultures of the region. Apartheid apologists had a stake in identifying and maintaining such 'traditional' groups. Just as apartheid theory denied the existence of permanent black residents in urban areas, apartheid culture refused to admit the existence of an emergent black urban culture.

The principles of apartheid culture infused the education system (both bantu education and Christian National Education), the mass media (radio, TV, and newspapers), and all state-linked structures involved in funding the arts.

Of course, people developed their own forms of cultural expression despite official attitudes and structures, and the lack of resources. With the earliest shanty-towns and illegal shebeens came marabi and the roots of South African jazz, a tradition which produced a number of internationally known musicians.

In the 1950s, writers centred around *Drum* magazine developed a distinctive style of prose writing. The early 1970s saw a wealth of poetry and theatre linked to the student and black consciousness movements. Directly tied to political defiance, songs such as Meadowlands (protesting the 1950s Sophiatown removals) and the poetry and songs of Vuyisile Mini (a trade union and ANC leader executed for sabotage in 1964) became part of the 'folk culture' of the townships.

Culture as a 'weapon of struggle'

In the 1980s cultural activists began to develop what was termed 'people's culture' as a tool for mass mobilisation against apartheid. The concept was first publicly adopted in 1982 in Gaborone, at a conference entitled 'Culture and Resistance'. Taking a stand against the notion of the elite artist working in isolation, the conference called on cultural workers to commit themselves to the oppressed communities, and to explore the expressions, realities and demands of grassroots South African society.

The birth of the UDF in 1983 provided a platform – often literally – for this vibrant cultural voice. The resurgence of mass organisation brought a new mood of empowerment, creating an environment alive to the importance and potentials of cultural work. Hundreds of community events opened up the space for untold numbers to share in some of the creativity, imagination, humour and defiance so alive beneath the squalor, pain and violence of the townships.

Struggles within various sectors of the democratic movement were taken up in cultural campaigns. The End Conscription Campaign deliberately worked to build an anti-military culture, encouraging anti-war murals, rock groups, and theatre. Similar strategies were used to highlight the women's struggle.

The founding of the Durban Cultural Workers Local in 1984 sounded the first note of the national worker cultural movement. Located within the black trade unions, and often inspired by ongoing strikes and issues, this movement has produced hundreds of plays, a burst of oral poetry, dance, and film.

As people began to explore cultural forms to express their understandings and demands, a number of communities introduced art training programmes, such as the Community Arts Project in Cape Town, Funda Centre in Soweto and the Alexandra Art Centre outside Johannesburg. These centres played an important role in spreading art skills and ideas, and served as locations for cultural productions.

The power of cultural activity of the mass movement helped to weaken the state's stranglehold on broadcasting, record companies, and other cultural resources.

Establishment cultural institutions gradually and grudgingly began to use the language of popular culture. Thus, even the more formal spaces of culture saw a burgeoning of popular theatre, music, art and video. Museums, art festivals and literary competitions, once bastions of conservatism, have begun to look for broader participation in a bid to avoid being by-passed by history.

International outrage against apartheid led to

the cultural boycott. This had a two-fold effect: it provided more space for South African artists to develop their own styles and forms; and it acted as a focus for people within South Africa, making them more conscious of the negative influences of international culture that appeared here.

Repression

When the state cracked down on the mass movement in 1985, cultural activities assumed a new role. With political rallies, meetings, and banning of organisations, cultural occasions provided a forum for people to come together to witness their strength and celebrate their commitment. The state recognised the significance of this by banning many explicitly cultural events – the most prominent being the 1986 Cape Arts Festival. Its slogan would have been 'Towards a People's Culture'.

Cultural activists, like so many community workers, also suffered directly under the State of Emergency. Police raided community art programmes, and detained students and teachers. Books were banned and toyi-toyi was declared a revolutionary activity. Many cultural workers went into hiding.

By 1987 the pressures on the mass movement had left many structures barely functional. The UDF Cultural Desk was launched to facilitate the growth and organisation of local culture. It also sought to assist in clarifying and implementing the international cultural boycott.

The Desk's first job was to co-ordinate the conference entitled 'Culture in Another South Africa' (CASA). CASA brought exiled and internal progressive workers together in Amsterdam, Holland, to talk, to debate the direction of progressive culture.

The conference endorsed earlier positions on the need to build cultural organisations. It also changed the thrust of the cultural boycott, calling for cultural exchange between the international community and the oppressed people of South Africa, while maintaining a ban on those who were not prepared to take a stand against the apartheid system.

The event served as an important rallying point, and a showcase for the range of exciting progressive cultural work being done in South Africa. But cultural workers returning from CASA came back to repression and the on-going State of Emergency: many of the resolutions taken there are yet to be fulfilled.

Culture in a future South Africa

South African society finds itself poised on the edge of vast and uncertain changes. Cultural workers aligned to the democratic movment have been forced to look again at the place of culture within their communities, and to evaluate their work in terms of what they can contribute to a future society.

Albie Sachs, in a paper to an ANC cultural forum in 1989, challenged cultural workers to produce more works 'which by-pass, overwhelm and ignore apartheid'. He echoed the sentiments of other cultural workers, that slogans and overt political content by themselves cannot replace the subtlety, complexity and ambiguity that effective cultural work demands.

What is the role of culture in the period of transition? How can our work help 'open wide the doors of culture?' How can we correct a situation where for so long the state has pumped resources into facilities and opportunities for the minority alone? And what kind of cultural work is needed to end the ethos of oppression, to go beyond angry reaction to apartheid? How do we start building that boldness, creativity and self-confidence needed to transform South African society?

The discussion and debate on the role of culture in building our new society is likely to continue long into the future.

One thing is certain: progressive cultural workers will be as important in the unfolding of a new South Africa as they have been in breaking down the oppressive and racist consciousness of the old South Africa. They will be creating images – through plays, poetry, music and graphics – that animate, inspire and encourage people to be the active authors of their own future. ❏

286 1986. Calling all cultural workers to participate in the first major arts festival organised by the democratic movement inside the country – the festival was banned by the state.
*Silkscreened poster produced for the Arts Festival Committee, Cape Town
Grey, yellow, black and red*

287 1986. Exhibition of visual art as part of the Arts Festival.
Silkscreened poster produced for the Arts Festival Committee, Cape Town
Black, red, ochre, grey and purple

288 1986. The logo of the Arts Festival.
Offset litho poster produced for the Arts Festival Committee, Cape Town
Black, red and green

289 1989. The excitement experienced at a union cultural event.
Offset litho poster produced by COSATU for FAWU, Johannesburg
Black

290 1984. Culture in Alexandra to raise funds for the youth.
Silkscreened poster produced by AYCO at STP, Johannesburg
Blue, green, red and yellow (marbled)

291 1986. A call to attend a community market to raise money for the unemployed.
Silkscreened poster produced by CAP, Cape Town
Blue and red

292 1984. Youth from the coloured area of Eldorado Park propose a 'lekker' (Afrikaans for nice, great, enjoyable, etc) disco to raise money.
Silkscreened poster produced by Eldo's Youth at STP, Johannesburg
Red and blue (marbled)

293 1987. Cultural exhibition to celebrate the tenth anniversary
of the Community Arts Project.
Silkscreened poster produced by CAP, Cape Town
Black, green, yellow and red

294 1983. The city council refused permission for JODAC to use the hall. The concert was cancelled.
Silkscreened poster produced by JODAC, Johannesburg
Green on brown wrapping paper

CONCERT

NAMIBIA

POETRY MIME
AND DANCE TO

MA-PANTSULA

CHERRY FACED LURCHERS

SPECTRES

SOFTIES

R3 CIVIC METHODIST CHURCH
NEXT TO YMCA
FROM 7PM SAT 30 JUNE

ECC
End Conscription Campaign

FORCES FAVOURITES

11 bands play against the Call-up

RECORD TAPE End Conscription

SHIFTY
ECC
End Conscription Campaign

296 1985.
Advertisement for
anti-conscription
tape and record.
*Silkscreened
poster produced at
STP by ECC,
Johannesburg
Red, yellow and
blue*

295 1984. Poster for a concert
which formed part of a
week-long focus on Namibia.
*Silkscreened poster produced at
STP by ECC, Johannesburg
Black and red*

297 c1985. Focusing on
women's issues.
*Silkscreened poster produced by the
WWM, Johannesburg
Black, blue and yellow*

WOMEN
MAKE THE
MUSIC

WITH Edi Niederlander
Kate Normington
Khaki Monitor
Natalie Gamsu
AND OTHERS

WITS
BOZZOLI SAT 12 SEPT
R5
Issued by Wits Women's Movement

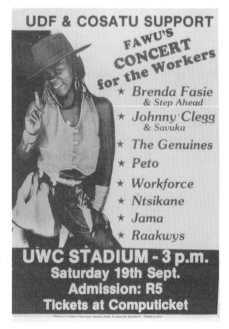

UDF & COSATU SUPPORT

FAWU'S
CONCERT
for the Workers

★ Brenda Fasie
& Step Ahead

★ Johnny Clegg
& Savuka

★ The Genuines

★ Peto

★ Workforce

★ Ntsikane

★ Jama

★ Raakwys

UWC STADIUM - 3 p.m.
Saturday 19th Sept.
Admission: R5
Tickets at Computicket

298 c1987. UDF, COSATU and local
musicians give support to FAWU.
*Offset litho poster produced by FAWU,
Cape Town
Red and yellow*

299 1987. Concert in support of people detained under security laws.
Silkscreened poster produced by Bonteheuwel Youth at CAP, Cape Town
Black

300 1985. UDF held People's Festivals in 1984 and 1985, winning the support and participation of mainstream musicians.
Offset litho poster produced by UDF, Johannesburg
Black, red and yellow

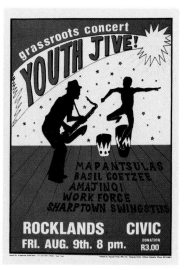

301 1987. The Progressive Arts Project attempted to organise cultural workers into collective action.
Offset litho poster produced by PAP, Johannesburg
Black

302 c1986. Local bands play at a concert organised by a community newspaper.
Offset litho poster produced by Grassroots Publications, Cape Town
Black and red

303 1985. The music of resistance will overcome militarisation.
Offset litho poster produced by ECC, Cape Town
Black and yellow

304 1986. A consciousness-raising film festival for those opposed to military conscription.

Offset litho poster produced by ECC, Cape Town
Black, red and green

305 1988. Repression under a monstrous PW Botha fails to silence the laughter of the people.
Offset litho poster produced by the Baxter Theatre, Cape Town
Black, blue and pink

306 1985. Exhibition of anti-militarism posters.
Silkscreened poster produced by ECC at CAP, Cape Town
Black, red and yellow

307 1989. Advert for an Arts Festival exhibition.
Silkscreened poster produced by CAP, Cape Town
Black and yellow

308 1987. Photographic exhibition of children as victims of, and participants in, the struggle for freedom.
Offset litho poster produced by Afrapix
Black and red

309 c1986. Sacked BTR Sarmcol workers stage a play,
The Long March, to illustrate their struggle against the bosses.
Silkscreened poster produced by Sarmcol workers at SAWCO, Howick, Natal
Black, red, brown and grey

310 1989. Another play produced by the fired workers of Sarmcol.
Offset litho poster produced by COSATU for NUMSA
Black, red and yellow

311 1986. Sarmcol workers' play advertised in Afrikaans.
Silkscreened poster produced by SAWCO, Natal
Black and red

312 c1985. Theatre is a means of liberation.
Offset litho poster produced by Action Workshop, Cape Town
Black

313 1987. COSATU brings home the importance of culture to workers at their cultural day.
Offset litho poster produced by COSATU, Johannesburg
Black, red and yellow

First half of the programme includes
music, mime and dance by Jazzart

When: Sun 27 Aug   8pm
Sat 2 Sept   8pm
Sun 3 Sept   3pm & 8pm

Where: CAP, 106 Chapel St, Woodstock

Cost: R2.00

Note: Performances start promptly

314 1989. Cultural performance
highlighting rejection of the tri-cameral
parliamentary system.
Silkscreened poster produced by CAP,
Cape Town
Green

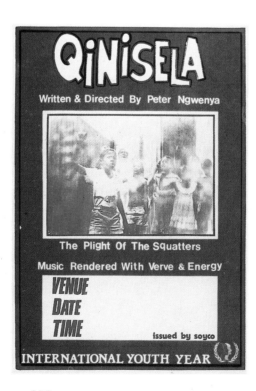

315 1985. A play about the struggle of
squatters, produced to commemorate
International Youth Year.
Silkscreened poster produced by SOYCO
at STP, Johannesburg
Blue and pink

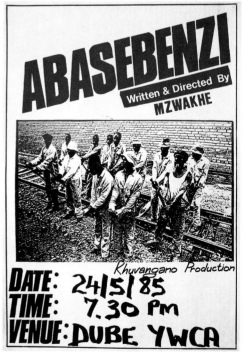

316 1985. A cultural group from
Soweto performed this play about
migrant workers.
Silkscreened poster produced by
Khuvangano Productions at STP,
Johannesburg
Black and red

317 1983. A performance on struggle in South Africa and the need for action.
Silkscreened poster produced by Action Workshop at CAP, Cape Town
Black, red and yellow

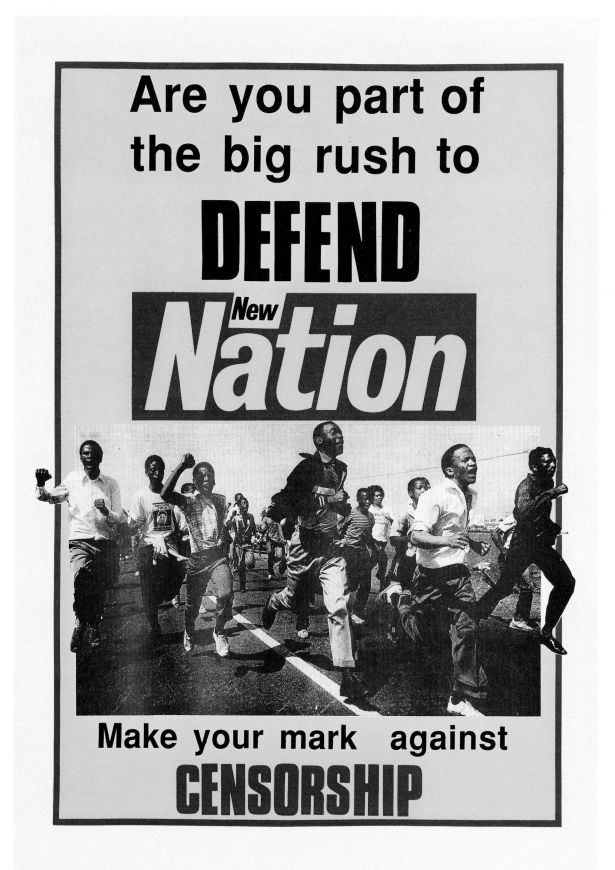

318 1988. Billboard poster calling for opposition to censorship and support for *New Nation*, a progressive newspaper muzzled by the state.
Offset litho poster produced by New Nation, Johannesburg
Black, red and yellow

319 1987. ACAG challenges the detention of progressive journalists.
Offset litho poster produced by ACAG, Johannesburg
Black

320 1989. 'We speak for the community. Help us in our struggle.' (translation from Afrikaans) *Namaqua Nuus* is a community newspaper in Namibia.
Silkscreened poster produced at CAP, Cape Town
Red

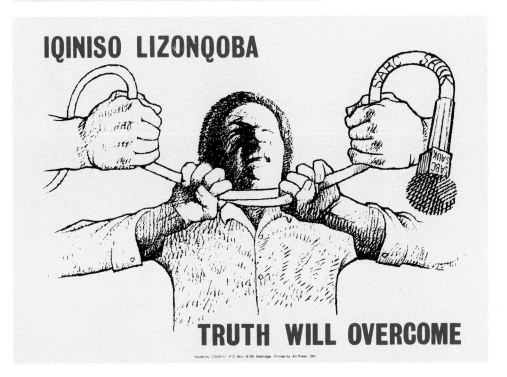

321 1986. Poster illustrating the incapacitation of organisations by the SABC's biased reporting.
Offset litho poster produced by COSATU
Black and red

322 1988. Rally to protest state interference in freedom of the press. *Offset litho poster produced by ADJ, Johannesburg Black, red and yellow*

323 1986. A challenge to the Department of Information's view of itself as an impartial channel of information. *Silkscreened poster produced by NUSAS, Johannesburg Black*

324 c1989. The media protests against restrictions on press freedom under the States of Emergency of the late 1980s. *Offset litho poster produced by SASPU, Johannesburg Black and red*

325 c1989. A call to journalists to oppose state attempts to muzzle the press. *Offset litho poster produced by East Cape News Agencies, Eastern Cape Black and yellow*

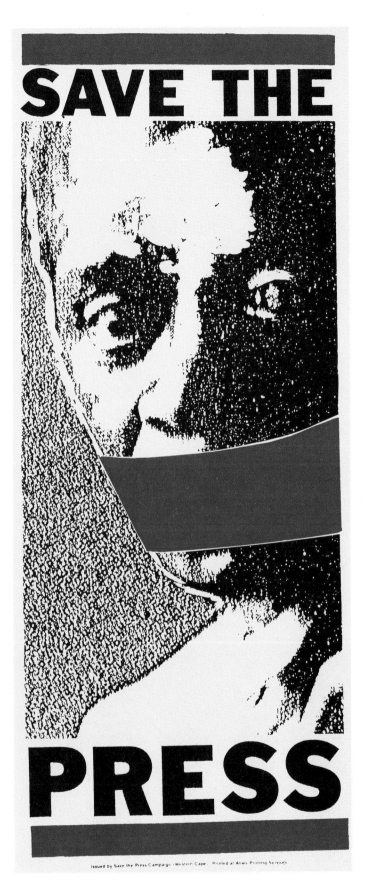

326 c1989. The struggle for a free media continues.
Offset litho poster issued by the Save the Press Campaign
(Western Cape)
Black and red

327 1985. The press is gagged – so find
other ways to get your message across.
Silkscreened poster produced at STP,
Johannesburg
Black

Afterword

Towards the end of November 1986, whilst I was an inmate of Johannesburg Prison, I was taken under escort to Hillbrow for a medical appointment. As the police van I was in parked outside the doctor's rooms, hundreds of singing and slogan-shouting workers marched by, defiantly holding aloft a huge COSATU banner. In the sea of faces, I saw several bright red and yellow posters which bore, in bold, black lettering, the words: 'We demand a living wage!'

To me, the scene I had just witnessed, as I got out of the police van and walked, chained in leg-irons like a dangerous beast, across the pavement and into the doctor's rooms, was a great morale booster. What I had just seen appealed directly to my heart and mind, and reminded me that the cause for which I was in prison was a just one.

As soon as I completed writing my University of South Africa (UNISA) examinations a few days later, I started work on a series of posters, which I drew on the inside covers of examination writing pads.

On 8 January 1987, the 65th anniversary of the founding of the African National Congress, I hung up the posters just a few minutes before our clandestine commemoration service was to take place in the cell where we normally met for political discussions. Spontaneous and joyous shouts of 'Amandla!' and 'Viva ANC–SACP-COSATU!' rang out as comrades saw the colourful posters. It was clear from the immediate response of all present that the posters had succeeded in their objective to communicate.

Poster produced by Dikobe wa Mogale Ben Martins while he was in prison, and printed by the ANC in 1991.

This book presents a meaningful and inspiring sample of posters produced and published by the Congress Movement. It graphically shows us the manner in which Congress organisations communicated with the oppressed people, politicising them, and pointing out political campaigns to be engaged in and tasks to be done; in sum: asking for co-operation and total commitment to the struggle.

Just paging through the posters reproduced in this book will enable us to revisit the challenges and the struggles that our people faced so dramatically and bravely in the 1980s. These posters bear testimony to the flexibility in their approach, and the issues around which they campaigned. The cumulative effect of these posters evokes an extreme sense of urgency coupled with a drive to mobilise feeling and reason, and to put both to the service of day-to-day struggles through concrete action.

But the last poster has not been printed yet. Today, the interests and perceptions of South Africans are changing as we move towards the so-called New South Africa. The present state of flux has produced more critically-minded viewers, who make greater demands on the poster artist–cum–activist. Artistic techniques are necessary and appreciated, but it is not enough to be merely technically competent. In order to keep abreast with the demands of the times, poster-makers will have to look at the world anew. We must strive for originality and novelty in our images, a balance in form and content, but above all, we must retain the strength that marks many of these posters: their power to communicate effectively by fusing aesthetic validity with simplicity so as to express an idea in the most incisive way.

Dikobe wa Mogale Ben Martins

List of acronyms

ACA *Athlone Civic Association*
ACTSTOP *Act to Stop Evictions*
ADAC *Ad Hoc Detention Action Committee*
ADJ *Association of Democratic Journalists*
ANC *African National Congress*
Anti-PC *Anti-Presidents Council*
AYCO *Alexander Youth Congress*
AZASO *Azanian Students' Organisation*
BLA *Black Local Authorities*
BEYCO *Belgravia Youth Congress*
BSIC *Black Students' Interim Committee*
BSS *Black Students' Society*
CAP *Community Arts Project*
CASA *Culture in Another South Africa*
CAYCO *Cape Youth Congress*
CCAWUSA *Commercial, Catering and Allied Workers' Union of South Africa* [1]
CLOWU *Clothing Workers' Union*
CNETU *Council of Non-European Trade Unions*
COD *Congress of Democrats*
COSAS *Congress of South African Students*
COSATU *Congress of South African Trade Unions*
CRADORA *Cradock Residents Association*
DAG *Detainees Action Group*
DESCOM *Detainees Support Committee*
DETU *Democratic Teachers' Union*
DPSC *Detainees Parents Support Committee*
ECC *End Conscription Campaign*
ELPTU *East London Professional Teachers' Union*
ERAPO *East Rand People's Organisation*
FAWU *Food and Allied Workers' Union*
FCCA *Federation of Cape Civic Associations*
FCWU *Food and Canning Workers' Union*
FEDSAW *Federation of South African Women*
FEDTRAW *Federation of Transvaal Women*
FFF *Five Freedoms Forum*
FOSATU *Federation of South African Trade Unions*
GAYCO *Gardens Youth Congress*
HCA *Huhudi Civic Association*
HIC *Health Information Centre*
HUYO *Huhudi Youth Organisation*
ICU *Industrial and Commercial Workers' Union*
IYY *International Youth Year*
JMC *Joint Management Centre*
JODAC *Johannesburg Democratic Action Committee*
JUWRC *Joint Union Workers' Representative Committee*
KRO *Krugersdorp Residents Organisation*
MARS *Media and Research Services*
MAWU *Metal and Allied Workers' Union*
MDM *Mass Democratic Movement*
MK *Umkhonto we Sizwe*
NACTU *National Council of Trade Unions*
NAMDA *National Medical and Dental Association*
NANSCO *Namibian National Students Congress*
NANSO *Namibian National Students Organisation*
NECC *National Education Crisis Committee* [2]
NRC *National Reception Committee* [3]
NUM *National Union of Mineworkers*
NUMSA *National Union of Metalworkers of South Africa*
NUNW *National Union of Namibian Workers*
NUSAS *National Union of South African Students*
PAC *Pan-Africanist Congress*

PAP *Progressive Arts Project*
PEBCO *Port Elizabeth Black Civic Organisation*
PHT *Popular History Trust*
POTWA *Post and Telecommunication Workers' Union*
PPWAWU *Paper, Printing, Wood and Allied Workers' Union* [4]
RAM *Rock Against Management*
RAWU *Retail and Allied Workers' Union*
RMC *Release Mandela Committee*
RRA *Rockville Residents Association*
SAAWU *South African Allied Workers' Union*
SACP *South African Communist Party* [5]
SACPO *South African Coloured People's Organisation*
SACTU *South African Congress of Trade Unions*
SADF *South African Defence Force*
SADWU *South African Domestic Workers' Union*
SAHA *South African History Archive*
SAIC *South African Indian Congress*
SAMWU *South African Municipal Workers' Union*
SANNC *South African Native National Congress* [6]
SASDU *South African Scooter Drivers' Union*
SASPU *South African Students Press Union*
SAYCO *South African Youth Congress*
SCA *Soweto Civic Association*
SFAWU *Sweet, Food and Allied Workers' Union*
SOYCO *Soweto Youth Congress*
SPP *Surplus Peoples Project*
SPCC *Soweto Parents Crisis Committee*
STP *Screen Training Project*
SUCA *Students Union for Christian Action*
SWAPO *South West African People's Organisation*
TAG *Technical Advice Group*
TCA *Tembisa Civic Association*
TGWU *Transport and General Workers' Union*
TIC *Transvaal Indian Congress*
TOPS *The Other Press Service*
UCT *University of Cape Town*
UDF *United Democratic Front*
WAR *Women Against Repression*
WECTU *Western Cape Teachers' Union*
WITS *University of the Witwatersrand*
WPCC *Western Province Council of Churches*
WPGWU *Western Province General Workers' Union*

NOTES

1. The union has since merged with other unions in this sector and is now called South African Commercial and Catering Workers' Union (SACCAWU).
2. After 2 February 1990 the organisation was renamed the National Education Co-ordinating Committee (NECC).
3. Formed on the release of Walter Sisulu and other long serving political prisoners to welcome and celebrate their return to society. It disbanded after the unbanning of the ANC and other political organisations.
4. Formerly Paper, Wood and Allied Workers' Union (PWAWU), it became PPWAWU when it merged with the National Union of Printing and Allied Workers (NUPAWO).
5. Formerly Communist Party of South Africa (CPSA). Disbanded in 1950, it relaunched in 1953 as the SACP.
6. The SANNC, formed in 1912, was the forerunner of the ANC.

Select chronology

1910. May 31. *Britain hands over power to white Union of South Africa.*
1912. Jan 8. *ANC (SANNC) founding conference*
1919. Jan 7. *ICU founded.*
1921. Jul 29. *Formation of CPSA.*
1946. Aug 12. *Strike by 100 000 African miners.*
1950. May 7. *CPSA disbands in anticipation of being banned.*
1952. Jun 26. *Defiance Campaign.*
1953. July 14. *SACP succeeds CPSA*
1954. Apr 17. *Formation of FEDSAW.*
1955. Feb 15. *60 000 Africans removed at gunpoint from Johannesburg's Western Areas under the Group Areas Act.*
Mar 5. *SACTU formed.*
Jun 26. *Congress of the People. Declared SA Freedom Day.*
Aug 9. *20 000 women march on Pretoria. Declared South African Women's Day*
1960. Mar 21. *Sharpeville massacre where 69 people were killed in pass law protest.*
Mar 28. *Oliver Tambo leaves SA to establish ANC mission in exile.*
Apr 30. *South Africa's first State of Emergency declared; over 2 000 detained.*
1961. Dec 11. *Chief AJ Luthuli, president of ANC, awarded Nobel Peace Prize.*
Dec 16. *First armed actions by MK. Declared Heroes Day.*
1963. Oct 5. *Looksmart Ngudle, the first political prisoner tortured to death.*
1964. Jun 12. *Rivonia trial ends. Life sentences for Mandela, Sisulu, Mbeki, Goldberg, Kathrada, Mlangeni, Mhlaba, Motsoaledi.*
Nov 6. *SACTU activists Vuyisile Mini, Wilson Khayinga, Zinakile Mkaba hanged.*
1965. Feb 9. *'I believe in the supremacy of the white man over his people in his own territory and I am prepared to maintain it by force'. – John Vorster in parliament.*
1973. Feb 3. *First large contingents of South African conscripts sent to Namibia.*
Feb 20. *Strike wave launched in Natal, opening a new wave of trade union organisation throughout the country.*
1975. Oct 19. *SA invades Angola.*
1976. Jun 16. *Soweto uprising. Declared SA Youth Day.*
1977. Sept 12. *Steve Biko dies in police detention.*
Oct 19. *18 organisations and two newspapers banned.*
1979. Apr 6. *Solomon Mahlangu hanged. He said: 'My blood shall nourish the tree that will bear the fruits of freedom'.*
1980. Apr 18. *Zimbabwe independence.*
1981. Jan 30. *ANC and SACTU exiles massacred at Matola in Mozambique by SA army.*
June 1. *MK attacks Sasol fuel complex.*
Dec 20. *Griffiths Mxenge, UDF lawyer, hacked to death by apartheid agents.*
1982. Feb 5. *Death of Neil Aggett in police detention.*
Aug 17. *Assassination of Ruth First in Maputo by parcel bomb.*
Dec 9. *SA raid into Lesotho kills 42.*
1983.June 9. *MK cadres Mosololi, Motaung,*

Moegerane executed.
Aug 20. *Launch of UDF in Cape Town.*
1984. Mar 16. *Nkomati Accord, non-aggression treaty, signed by SA and Mozambique.*
Jun 28. *Assassination of Jeanette Schoon and daughter Katryn by parcel bomb sent by SA agents.*
Aug 22. *Coloured elections for tri-cameral parliament yield 17% poll.*
Sept 3. *Vaal uprising.*
Dec 11. *Archbishop Desmond Tutu awarded Nobel Peace Prize.*
1985. Jan 2. *First National ECC Conference at Botha's Hill, Durban*
Mar 21. *Langa Massacre: 20 shot dead by police in Uitenhage.*
May 19. *SADF raids Harare, Gaborone and Lusaka.*
Jun 14. *SADF raids Gaborone, killing 12.*
Jul 20. *Funeral of Cradock 4.*
Jul 21. *Second State of Emergency declared.*
Aug 1. *Victoria Mxenge assassinated at her home in Durban.*
Oct 18. *Malesela Benjamin Moloise executed in defiance of international calls for clemency.*
Oct 26. *State of Emergency extended to entire country.*
Dec 1. *Formation of COSATU.*
1986. Jun 12. *Third State of Emergency declared.*
Oct 19. *President Samora Machel of Mozambique killed in plane crash.*
Dec 11. *Dr Fabian and Florence Ribiero assassinated.*
1987. May 7. *COSATU headquarters bombed.*
1988. Jan 19. *ANC headquarters in Lusaka bombed by SA.*
Feb 21. *SA army defeated after six months battle against Angolan troops backed by Cuban solidarity forces.*
Mar 29. *Dulcie September, ANC chief representative in Paris, assassinated by SA agents.*
Aug 23. *Khotso House, headquarters of SA Council of Churches blown up.*
1989. May 1. *David Webster killed on May Day.*
Sept 1. *Defiance campaign against banning and restriction orders and against segregation in hospitals and other facilities.*
Oct 15. *Walter Sisulu and other Rivonia trialists released.*
Dec 10. *Conference for a Democratic Future.*
1990. Feb 2. *ANC legalised after 30 years (SACP, PAC and 70 other organisations also unbanned).*
Feb 11. *Nelson Mandela released.*
Mar 21. *Namibia Independence Day.*
May 2. *First meeting between ANC and apartheid government; ends with joint commitment to peaceful negotiations.*
Jul 29. *Public relaunch of SACP at Soweto rally.*
Aug 1. *ANC/MK suspends armed actions after 29 years.*
Aug-Sept. *Over 750 people killed in Aug-Sept wave of violence unleashed against the ANC as part of a strategy of destabilisation.*